Praise for Carol Orsborn's Books

THE YEAR 1 SAVED MY (downsized) SOUL
"What a ride! With humility, humor and courageous honesty, Carol Orsborn invites us along on her journey from paralyzing fear through surrender to wisdom. What the author shares about facing the unknown and growing to embrace uncertainty will appeal to everyone who worries about losing a job or losing faith." Patti Breitman, author, How to Say No Without Feeling Guilty

THE ART OF RESILIENCE
"A wonderful new book about remembering the most important thing in life—love." Gerald G. Jampolsky, author, Love Is Letting Go of Fear

INNER EXCELLENCE
"One of the cornerstones of building the organization of the future will be distinguishing intrinsic from extrinsic motivation. Orsborn's concept of inner excellence is an excellent place for managers seriously interested in cultivating intrinsic motivation to begin their quest." Peter Senge, author, The Fifth Discipline

HOW WOULD CONFUCIUS ASK FOR A RAISE?
"Fresh and funny and spiritual...an easily accessible guide for helping us live fuller lives. Supremely useful." John Naisbitt, author, Global Paradox

RETURN FROM EXILE
"I hope many readers will follow Carol Orsborn on her spiritual journey and will learn something about their own souls in the process." Harold S. Kushner, author, When Bad Things Happen to Good People

The Year I Saved My
(downsized) Soul

Books by Carol Orsborn

THE ART OF RESILIENCE

SOLVED BY SUNSET

HOW WOULD CONFUCIUS ASK FOR A RAISE?

INNER EXCELLENCE

INNER EXCELLENCE AT WORK

NOTHING LEFT UNSAID

THE SILVER PEARL (with Dr. Jimmy Laura Smull)

ENOUGH IS ENOUGH

SPEAK THE LANGUAGE OF HEALING (with Dr. Susan Kuner et al.)

RETURN FROM EXILE

BOOM (with Mary Brown)

AS GOOD AS IT GETS

TRUST, INC. (with Judith Rogala)

The Year I Saved My (downsized) Soul

A Boomer Woman's Search for Meaning...and a Job

CAROL ORSBORN, PH.D.

vn
books

Vibrant Nation Books, Louisville

Vibrant Nation Books
111 West Washington St., #400
Louisville, KY 40202

DEDICATION

IN MEMORIAM, FR. GREG CONNELL

MAY HE REST IN PEACE

ACKNOWLEDGEMENTS

The I Ching

Vanderbilt Divinity School

Stephen Reily and the Vibrant Nation community

Penuel Ridge Retreat Center

Holy Spirit Retreat Center

Rabbi Abraham Joshua Heschel

May Sarton and all seekers of soul

My friends and muses, Patti Breitman and Linda Roghaar

My agent, who called forth the best in me, Beth Vesel

And as always: My beloved Dan, my children Grant and Jody, and our newest family member, Ginny

You have my deepest gratitude and appreciation.

AUTHOR'S NOTE

While based on actual events, this story is a tell-all about the state of my soul, not a tell-all about any individuals or companies for whom I have worked. With the exception of myself and my family members, the characters, timeline, geography, and any company or employer represented in the book either represent a composite or are entirely fictitious.

1

There are many reasons to write a memoir—to attempt to become immortal, to help people, to save the world, to make money, to find a cheap alternative to therapy. But I have found the most compelling reason of all: to save my soul.

Over the many decades of my life, I have been inspired by women writers like May Sarton, Elisabeth Ogilvie, Anne Morrow Lindbergh, and all of the gifted spiritual seekers whose words have spoken to me from the pages of books.

But while my heart responds to their writings as though I'd conceived them myself, they could not have been produced under circumstances more different from my own. These books were written by the ocean, in the forest, in the desert. These women asked themselves the big questions about friendship, purpose, the joys and limits of family, health, death, and the meaning of life. Their answers came from the whisperings of conches, the songs of nightingales in berried bushes, and the squish of mud beneath their toes.

I wanted to ask the big questions too. But I was not a beachcomber at the seashore but rather a senior executive in a global marketing firm on notice that unless she got her numbers up—fast!—hers would be among the next wave of pink slips. Fighting for my survival, I spent my days performing, explaining, and defending, my nights worrying and fretting. To find even a half-hour a night to think about and record the bigger picture of what was going on in my life, and to fight my way back towards what really matters, required more of me than I had to give.

But still I had to try.

2

It was just over a year ago that I found myself desperate to come to terms with turning one of those milestone birthday numbers that ends in a big zero while tottering miserably on the brink of a downsizing corporation.

It wasn't that long ago that marketing companies could afford to invest in "innovation officers" and "thought leaders," intellectual capital meant to enhance the corporation's reputation overall rather than add immediate dollars to the bottom line. In my case, I'd been recruited by Belle, a couple of years my senior, who somehow managed to pull off a look much edgier than mine. Handling one of the office's biggest pieces of business at the time, she had asked for another "grownup" with whom she could play. I had essentially been given to Belle as a gift.

Well before there'd been talk of recession, I was awarded

the job of co-leading a global practice dedicated to helping marketers understand, reach, and connect with Boomer women at the deepest levels, applying cutting-edge social sciences to brand marketing. In the beginning, integrating academia with marketing held the promise of making sense of my eclectic history. As a scholar, author, and business-woman, I forged a path through the seemingly disparate worlds of consumer products, religious history, adult psychology, and spiritual motivation.

For a while, the practice group not only embraced this potent mixture; it even offered space for mission. We would use everything we had both to win back the marketers who had abandoned the women of our generation to the stereotypes of the past and to garner us the respect that we deserve.

3

For many women of the Boomer generation, the dream has been to make one's living teaching at the graduate level or to support one's self writing books. Nobody I knew aspired to be working for a multinational company that was downsizing during the worst economy since the Great Depression, hanging onto one's job for dear life. The irony is that I'd been privileged to live the part of the dream that centered around teaching and writing—and yet, here I still sat in a wobbly chair under fluorescent lights, wondering if I'd somehow been living my life backwards.

It seems a lifetime ago when I landed my first job at 21. Days into my stint working for *The San Francisco Chronicle*, I realized that while the University of California, Berkeley, had given me a world-class education, it had also nurtured my tendencies to question the status quo. In doing so, it had made me virtually unemployable.

As soon as I could, I left to start my own business, a public relations consulting practice specializing in helping companies market to the teens and twenty-somethings of my generation. We were young Baby Boomers then, 80 million strong—the largest generational cohort in history—and the first time that consumers this young controlled enough discretionary wealth to attract the interest of mainstream marketers. Equipped with insider knowledge, I built my reputation helping "older" marketers in their thirties and forties navigate the alternative culture I was helping to create.

This consulting practice grew over the next twenty years, becoming one of the top independent firms of its kind in the country. But it wasn't long before the largest segment of the consumer base had passed the age 30 milestone and were ourselves on the way to middle age. There were new issues, challenges and opportunities related to the Boomer consumer as we progressed through life stages, all of which were being ignored by marketers, just at the moment I had become bored selling acne medicine to a new generation of teenagers.

With no place else to exercise my generational expertise, I started writing books geared to the women of my generation: book after book every year and a half or so. Each one was dedicated to solving whatever life stage challenges we were facing at the time. Finally 15 brightly colored covers decorated the fireplace mantel. I wrote early in the morning before work, at night while the kids were doing their homework, and on the weekends, especially when deadlines were approaching. This was more than an emotional release; it was a mission. I went on *Oprah* and *The Today Show*, won some national book awards and got letters from readers telling me I'd made an impact on their lives. That said, like most authors in my genre, I never sold enough books to make a living from my writing. And, too, I wanted something more.

Intending to leave both my public relations and writing careers behind, I invested seven years and briefcase loads of savings to earn my doctorate from Vanderbilt University. In the end, I hoped not only to explore the boundaries of human knowledge regarding the universal mysteries (which I did) but how to land a tenured track teaching post (which I didn't). The only ultimate secret that was revealed to me was that institutions were quite simply not offering the serious jobs to women "of a certain age."

Reviewing my vocational history, not on the distant shore of the professorship I'd dreamt about but as a corporate executive, I faced three decades or more of life, already unprepared financially for the future and now additionally saddled with educational loans. I took this job as what was to be the crowning glory of a succession of corporate positions to make up for lost time—and that was before the recession even hit. Now, sadly, the future looked not rosy, but pink, as in pink slip. I didn't dare consider the consequences if I were laid off.

4

When it came to my job history, I'd had a steep learning curve indeed. Not about my subject matter, but about corporate life. Even at its best, back in the beginning when times were flush, I had no crust. Having spent most of my career running my own business, writing books, and going to school, I was naïve about corporate dynamics—far more so than my years and title indicated.

I smarted over things that people did to each other in the corporate neighborhood, like fellow employees who secretly switched their desk chair for one that didn't wobble or lurch. For a couple of days, a few jobs back, not only my chair but my bookcase had gone entirely missing. As the economy eroded, having my furniture stolen was among the least of my worries. With the pressure to perform turned up to full throttle, corporations had proved to have the capacity to bring out the worst in even the best of us.

It tells you something about my mental state that the book on my bedside table was *Work's a Bitch and Then You Make It Work*. Author Andrea Kay offers "naked truths" about business.

Here are three of them:

You can be fired pretty much at any time for any reason....

You are not owed a good job and security for life....

Technology, a machine, or someone from China or India may replace you....

And then there's my own, the one that I consider to be the mother of all naked truths:

It's about the money, stupid!

I shelled out the bucks for the book, but I learned in the first few pages that I was not a candidate for what Kay calls an "attitude implant." I admit it. I had no intention of accepting any of the naked truths. Not a single one.

5

Back when corporations had enough money to reward favored managers with their choice of seasoned hires with degrees, books, and credentials, I was a dazzly thing on a hook and they couldn't resist gobbling. In my first corporate job interview, we had talked about capabilities and vision. We should have talked about the Chicago Haymarket Square Riot. In May, 1886, workers went on strike to demand an eight-hour day. People on all sides gave their lives when a bomb was lobbed into a group of policemen and the police fired into the crowd. As a result, workers formed unions to protect their rights. In a bygone era in which the economy depended on manufacturing products, the collective bargaining power of workers held real power in American business.

But we've now shifted from manufacturing to a

service-based economy. For the most part, things went all right for workers through the early 1980s as a result of the paternalistic view corporations had of their relationship with workers. Companies paid attention to things like pensions, health care, and balanced workloads. Workers, in exchange, were to provide the company with loyalty and dedicated service.

The recession of the early 1980s changed everything. Companies downsized their workforces, a process accelerated by the growing number of mergers and acquisitions. If you were lucky enough to keep your job, you also had to take on the duties of those who departed. As the years rolled along, technological innovation, coupled with the growing global marketplace, put pressure on individuals to work 24/7 for increasingly less security and fewer benefits.

The recent meltdown, the one that made the recession 25 years earlier look like kid stuff, officially ratified the trend: there would be no turning back to the good old days when companies had to give a hoot in order to compete. In its place was a new emphasis on billability, profitability numbers, and better income-to-expense ratios. Suddenly it didn't matter what the industry was, much less the corporation. More and more of my friends who still had jobs talked about tensions with fellow employees, who were increasingly pitted against one another, competing to be part of the shrinking pool of the working elite "fortunate" enough to have health care insurance.

When rumors of the first pink slips started circulating at my company, my more politically adept colleagues knew

21

how to make themselves invaluable. They appropriated successes and delegated failures. They championed work that promised high visibility and returns, whereas just about everything else trickled downstream, usually to the person with the chair that lurched most.

A friend of mine, approaching the holy grail of a fully vested retirement at a competitive firm, once confessed the secret of her corporate longevity to me: "If I'm just tearing up, I stay at my desk. If I'm sobbing, I get up and close the door. But I never let them see me wobble."

6

With every recession, talk of mission and vision gives way to abbreviations like P&L (profit and loss) and ROI (return on investment). Clearly, there are forces larger than any one of us at work. The economic meltdown sweeps over us all like a tsunami, and there is never enough time to do anything but take it all personally. Not long ago my emails had the potential to be powerful, catapulting others into action. Increasingly, my emails whimpered across electronic thresholds, eventually limping back home to me to die. Truly, I'd paid my dues, and now I'd expected to be at a point in my career where asking for stability and respect was not unreasonable.

All this was now beside the point. Yesterday's triumphs had already been forgotten, and I was being warned yet again that if I didn't start clocking in more billable hours, my days were numbered.

There it was: the convergence of the two major themes in my life in one cliché: my days were indeed numbered. I was in danger of losing this job: that was the first. My own personal mortality: that was the second. A milestone birthday: I caught myself thinking things like "Is this what it has all come to?" I was at least once again asking the big questions, but I was mortified to find myself doing so while howling at fluorescent lights instead of the moon. Definitively not the open-ended ambition of youth that actually believed that what she could do would make a difference, but rather a wizened calculation: how much more insecurity and pain would I be willing to suffer in exchange for keeping my health care coverage?

The answer was simple: everything and then some.

7

I was fully aware that my job could go away with the
snap of a balance sheet. So much for the myth of good,
hard work being rewarded. Dan and I had both worked
all our adult lives. But like so many of us, our retirement
investments had taken a hit—and now our online
checkbook was reminding us daily that we needed not one
but two incomes to make ends meet. I'd always assumed
that by now we would have accumulated enough to have the
economic wherewithal to choose whether to work, or not,
and certainly where, what, and how much.

When I was thinking rationally, I admitted that this
recession had dealt Boomers blows across the board—those
who were prudent and did everything their financial
advisors told them to do, as well as those who never really
believed they would live long enough to have to worry

about the future. But at the same time, it was hard not to take the instability of my job and our financial shortcomings as a sign of individual—or at least generational—failure.

I admit that it was hardly prudent of me to cash in our wedding presents in order to fund an extended backpacking tour of Europe. Then when I got my first job, my parents advised me to put aside money every month into a savings account that would compound geometrically. I ignored that advice, too. When we had kids, we did everything we could to cultivate their talents. From music lessons to drama camp, we wrote the checks trusting that somehow the future would take care of itself. Through all of life's twists and turns, when advertisements told me to put enough away for a rainy day, I was the kind of person who pulled her boots on, and went outside to splash around instead.

Anyway, I did make an investment. A good one. I became, in fact, fully vested in the things that really mattered to me. And even if in the confusion of worrying about keeping my job, I'd temporarily lost track of my soul—at least I knew how important it was to have one.

8

The hit our savings took was bad enough. But wouldn't it be sad, after a lifetime with so much effort extended, to also feel that when put to the test, my soul would come up short? Where was hope? Faith? Acceptance? Mortality is real, after all. And so are corporate earnings.

Weighted down by a growing list of mea culpas, I knew I had to do something redemptive or I would soon go under in a frenzy of self-pity. Late on a weekend afternoon, shadows growing tall in the dimming light, I decided to take my little puppy Lucky for a drive.

Lucky, part Yorkie and part Maltese (a "Morky"), loves nothing better than to sit on my lap, her head poking out the open window. If I couldn't lift my own spirits, at least

I could do something nice for her. In short order, we were loaded into the Saturn, Lucky's pepper-colored ears blowing wildly in the wind.

We took the skyline route along Mulholland and turned a corner on the winding road. Straight ahead, we found ourselves driving into a horizon ablaze with fire-orange and red with streaks of ocean blue. The colors irradiated the hills, sending plumes of pink cascading across the valley below. Awestruck by this blazing expanse, I remembered what it was like when I could set aside my everyday concerns and appreciate the luminous abundance of the universe. In the words of mystic philosopher Charles Kingsley, regardless of what was going on in my life at any given moment, I could suddenly be consumed with the innate feeling that everything I see has a meaning, if I could but understand it. "And this feeling of being surrounded with truths which I cannot grasp amounts to indescribable awe sometimes."

Every now and again, I have moments when I, too, sense myself to be part of a whole far greater than whatever challenges I am facing at the time. I have on occasion walked out into the night sky, consumed with humility at the infinite expanse of stars and planets. Standing in the presence of rainbows and waterfalls, I have felt how small I am and how immense the time and space within which we all dance for such a brief moment. On these occasions, I have found myself able to set aside primary concerns for security and turn my attention to forces urging my spirit to take flight.

But then again, I was having this moment of awe at 40

miles an hour, careening around a dead man's curve, trying to catch a quick glimpse of the rapidly climaxing sunset which had somehow slid into my rear view mirror.

I knew this was worth savoring if only I could find a place to pull over.

I couldn't.

9

The pressure to perform was taking on even more urgency as the convergence of pink slip and birthday cake lurked just around the corner. I was already one of the older people in the company. With women over 50 being laid off throughout the sector, I viewed this job as a slim, diminishing window of opportunity in which I could still be operating from such a lofty position. How long could I hang on? And if I were let go, how far and how fast could I slide? I already had friends who had been forced to give up health insurance. I knew family members who were moving in with one another to save on rent. Dan and I had resources, stashed away for a rainy day. But the economy had been raining for some time now, and suddenly I realized that in the best-case scenario, my umbrella was full of holes.

With my soul shivering in the storm, I felt the sudden urge to call Joan, formerly my therapist, now a life coach, seeking an emergency session. I needed help, both practical and metaphysical, hoping that somewhere, somehow there could be less worry and some kind of plan.

I liked it when Joan reinvented herself as a life coach, because before she mostly listened, looking wise and compassionate. Now she just told me what to do.

"Let me tell you the secret of the Samurai," she said. "The Samurai who was most willing to give up his life was the one most likely to win the struggle. Why? Because already reconciled with death, he had the least to lose. He could take the greatest risks, focus all of his energy on the attack and divert nothing for self-protection. He was the Samurai to be truly feared. This, in fact, is the essence of surrender—and what you are being called to do."

My preferred notion of surrender was more along the lines of going home and pulling the blankets over my head. Nevertheless, I trusted Joan and decided to give it a try. But where should I start, especially in light of my wobbly circumstances?

"Repeat after me," said Joan.

"*I understand that the economic conditions within which this company is operating have deteriorated, placing new and extreme pressures on us all. I will nevertheless do everything I can to succeed within this new reality.*

"*If they fire me, they fire me.*

"*I won't worry about the far future, but rather, stay focused on the here and now.*

"*After all, my big birthday is coming. Who knows if I'll*

live a short or long life? No control over that. Who knows if the economy will recover in time enough to make a difference for me? No control over that, either.

"All I can hope to control, however long I have and in whatever the economic circumstance, is whether I will bring my best or my worst to bear."

I admit that I left her office feeling better. But nevertheless, I wondered how I could continue paying for her services if I were to end up with a sword through my gut.

ALL YOU CAN HOPE TO CONTROL, HOWEVER LONG YOU HAVE AND IN WHATEVER THE CIRCUM-STANCES, IS WHETHER YOU WILL BRING YOUR BEST OR WORST TO BEAR.

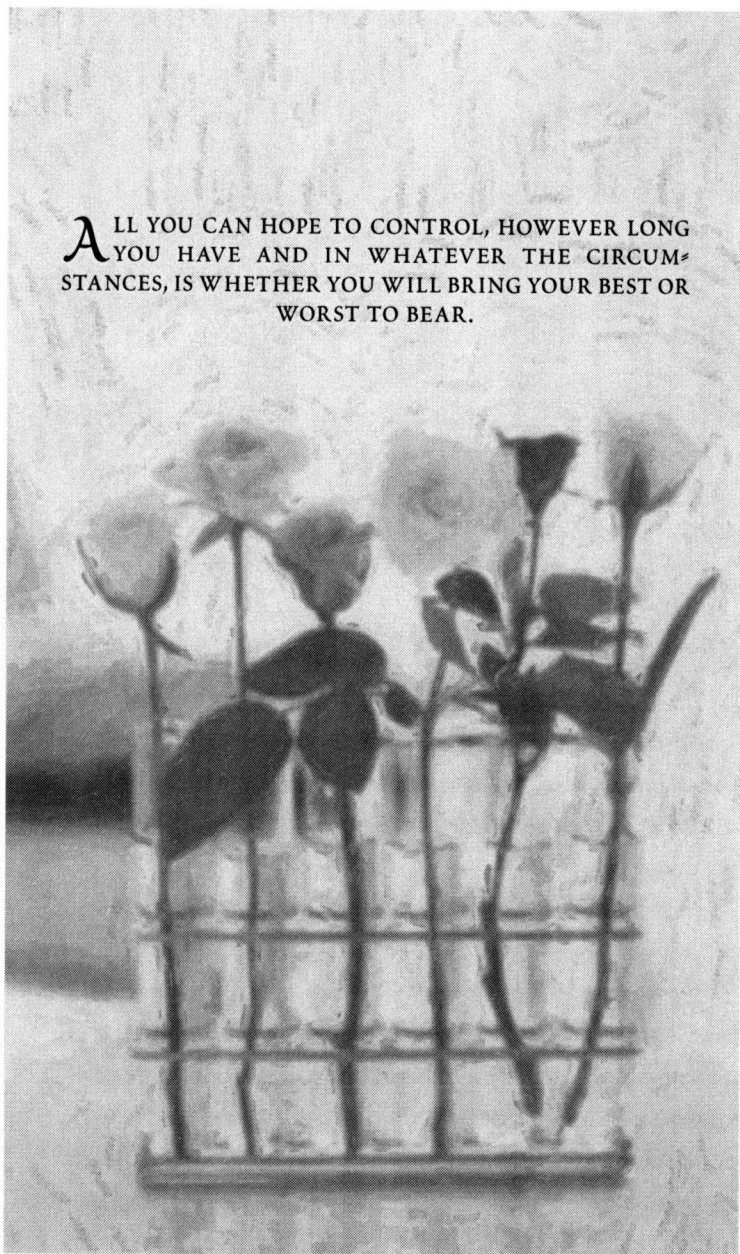

10

There are multiple paths to spiritual advancement. One is to quiet one's mind, to calm outside influences and nervous chatter so as to discern the deeper, stiller waters of one's soul. That is the path of the mystic who finds her refuge by escaping from the mainstream.

Surrender is the second, the willingness to fall on one's sword sacrificing self-protection for mission. It is the Samurai who takes his spot in the center of the economic hurricane, finding out what he is really made of. The Samurai does not take his commitment to responsibility and turn it against himself, feeling guilty for forces beyond his control. He does not allow ill winds to blow him off course, wasting vital energy that should be heading towards loftier goals. He does not let himself get swept swept up in a whirlwind of mea culpas.

Knowing all this, however, was not the same as doing it.

Thank God there was another path: that of the lump of coal, with at least the possibility of becoming forged by heat and pressure into a diamond. While I aspired to the glory of the Samurai, I had more in common with the lump of coal. For the truth was that within moments of leaving Joan's office, I was already once again roiling in insecurity about my job, worrying about not having saved enough for retirement, and suffering a general lack of faith in everything…especially myself.

The futility of the first path, refuge, was underlined when I lunched with my friend Fanny, who touched down in L.A. briefly from her new life in Bali. Dan and I had toyed with the urge to move to an exotic port around the same time Fanny and her husband Ben actually transplanted themselves. (For us it was to be Mexico.) In better times, we spent many an evening over sushi with Fanny and Ben at our favorite restaurant, talking through the possibilities. Dan and I went south of the border on a scouting trip. I saw a scorpion. And that was that.

They visited Bali and, on their first day there, found a tropical pavilion overlooking waterfalls. And it was cheap—so cheap that they could both quit their jobs, put in a marble bathroom, and hire so many house boys and girls that Fanny hadn't unpacked a single bag of groceries since.

But over an egg salad sandwich at her favorite deli in Los Angeles, Fanny told me that she was panicking because Ben had undergone emergency surgery, and suddenly they needed extra cash to pay for things like the airlift to

Thailand, where hospitals had the right medical equipment. Moreover, their investment rental in Santa Monica—the one they counted on to provide a steady stream of income—had burst a pipe and was sitting vacant. With Ben in recuperation, the only skill she could think of to call upon in Bali was one she'd thought she'd left behind years ago: administering colonics. Work of any sort is illegal for foreigners in Bali, even those who put marble bathrooms in their homes. She had quietly begun taking clients, constantly wary that any one of them could inform on her.

Sometimes, there is no escaping the pain. In fact, there are times when all we can do is remember to breathe.

T HERE ARE TIMES WHEN ALL YOU CAN DO IS
REMEMBER TO BREATHE.

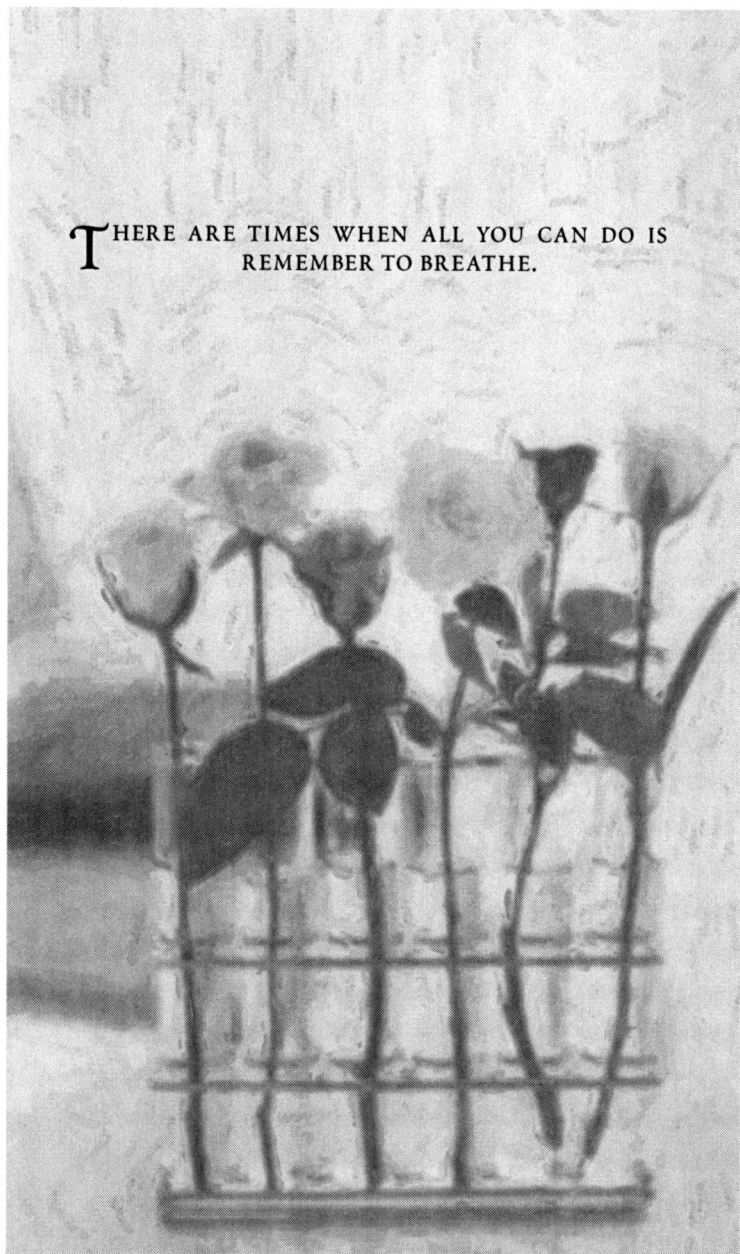

11

Belle called me to her office. We'd gotten some good news: the agency had received an invitation to pitch a global cracker company and the prospective client wanted not only to target moms of young children but the even larger chunk of their business, women over 50. Belle and I were invited to join the pitch team. Viewing this opportunity as my hope for salvation, I whole-heartedly launched into developing research and strategy that would make the connection with this critical target market. It was a welcome stroke to my ego that Belle had repeatedly told me that my intelligence, coupled with my credentials, would help provide the competitive edge over our contenders when it came to the Boomer-and-beyond demographic. While only one of us was to be physically in the room for the pitch, Belle was optimistic that if we landed this account, the heat would finally be off.

I brought everything I had to the proposal, daydreaming that when we won this account, the general manager would call me into the corner office and say: "Carol, I'm so sorry the company's been so hard on you. You're exactly what this company needs! Please forgive us. Not only are you off the pink slip list—but here's a bonus!" What a great birthday present that would be! Proof that my life had amounted to something, after all.

But alas, there was no summons, even as I kept my eye on the electronic calendar, knowing that Belle was at that very moment rehearsing the script for the part of the Power Point deck I'd helped write. Now the team would be figuring out who was going to be saying what. Now the calendar informed me she would be deep into the heart of the pitch itself.

Then I got a fresh email. From Belle, doing housecleaning on some minor billing effluvia relating to one of the speeches I had given last month, making sure I'd not only gotten the receipt from the airline for travel, but proof in the form of my credit card bill, that I'd actually flown.

"Aren't you in the middle of the pitch?" I emailed back.

"I was dis-invited," she responded. "The pitch team decided to build the proposal around mothers of young children."

If an email could have shrugged, it would have.

12

This turn of events shouldn't have been a complete surprise, as throughout the brainstorms and strategic development, the conversation had been dominated by the Alpha moms on the team who passionately debated things like whether children prefer crackers in the shape of elephants or lions. Meanwhile, I did have fresh insights for the 50+ part of the pitch. Defying the stereotypes, the latest research showed, for instance, that these 50+ women were online. At the peak of their careers, they had broken their teeth on the technology in the workplace, and highly motivated, they adopted new tools to foster and maintain intergenerational relationships with their children and grandchildren. They relied on the Internet for information on everything from the latest medical research and best travel deals to (yes!) the most nutritious brand of crackers. To reach this highly influential generation, we should be concentrating our efforts using the social networking websites targeted to Boomers and beyond. Surely this was the kind of fresh, creative thinking that would help us land the cracker client and save my job.

But then there was Belle giving me the update. Not only had she been dis-invited, but the team leading the new business charge, finding it impossible to fit everything in, had been forced to leave grand portions of women 50+ on the cutting-room floor.

So, anger! Anger at the stereotypes, invisibility and devaluation of aging women that persisted, despite all the hard evidence to the contrary. Anger at the young marketers on our end who could dismiss us and this key demographic so easily. Anger that I had not been utilized to my fullest to help us land the business. So much for my fantasy of redemption.

Nevertheless, the anger was liberating. As philosopher William James wrote, "Much of what we call evil…can so often be converted into a bracing and tonic good by a simple change of the sufferer's inner attitude from one of fear to one of fight; its sting so often departs and turns into relish when, after vainly to shun it, we agree to face about and bear it."

I had indeed been on the run, chased by worries about my job and chagrin over the lack of respect. Now I stopped and took a stand, finally turning the attention from feeling sorry for myself and back onto the mission. It was a good sign that the mission had survived, since that was the only piece of what was left of my vocation that nobody could take from me.

41

13

My birthday came and went, but this one felt different. I had, for starters, never imagined that I would be crossing this threshold so shy of my expectations of what my life was to be like at this serious-sounding age. I ricocheted between anger and denial, still holding a dim birthday-candle-sized hope that we would land the cracker company and there would be just enough crumbs left over for me to justify my salary. But frankly, I was unnerved by an email from Belle that arrived just before the pink cake. My boss was asking me how many billable hours she could count on me for this week (and the answer was none).

After the office party, she apologized for being distracted, confessing that if the agency didn't land the cracker account, she'd been told that "a price would have to be paid." Was that price me? She didn't say and I didn't dare ask. The question lingered, however, for after the cake, I caught a glimpse of her heading up to the general manager's office. As the door slammed shut, I remembered Joan's session on surrender. Now was my moment to find out what I was really made of. Was I the kind of person who became a victim of circumstances or the kind who had it in her to thrive, regardless of what came her way?

I knew what I wanted. I hoped to take my cue from Jacob, son of Isaac, who found his answer on the banks of the Jabbok River. In the story from the Hebrew Scriptures, Jacob had reached midlife, having devoted a lifetime to winning God's favor, but his efforts were flawed. He cheated his brother Esau of his birthright, then left home to make his fortune, thinking material comfort would bring him the blessing he sought. But when midlife came, he began to long for the one thing all his clever manipulations failed to bring him: reconciliation.

He set out for his childhood home, willing to do whatever it took to rectify his past. Jacob knew what he wanted and he was going for it, but along the way, on the banks of the Jabbok River, he was met by an agent of God who engaged him in a life-or-death struggle. All night long, Jacob wrestled the angel on the river bank. In the heat of the battle, Jacob's hip was seriously injured. But when morning dawned, Jacob finally received what he'd sought all his life: God's blessing (Genesis 32.22–32).

Jacob learned that it is the willingness to engage in the struggle for what really matters that merits God's intervention—not how deserving we think we are, nor whether we manage to emerge unwounded. Only when one answers the summons to rise to the occasion, putting everything on the line, do we even have the chance of encountering the essence of the divine. This is the source of raw creativity out of which new possibilities arise.

Out of depths unknown, a thought spontaneously occurred to me. The time had come to begin quietly looking for another job.

IT IS THE WILLINGNESS TO ENGAGE IN THE STRUGGLE FOR WHAT REALLY MATTERS THAT MERITS GOD'S INTERVENTION—NOT HOW DESERVING YOU THINK YOU ARE, NOR WHETHER YOU MANAGE TO EMERGE UNWOUNDED.

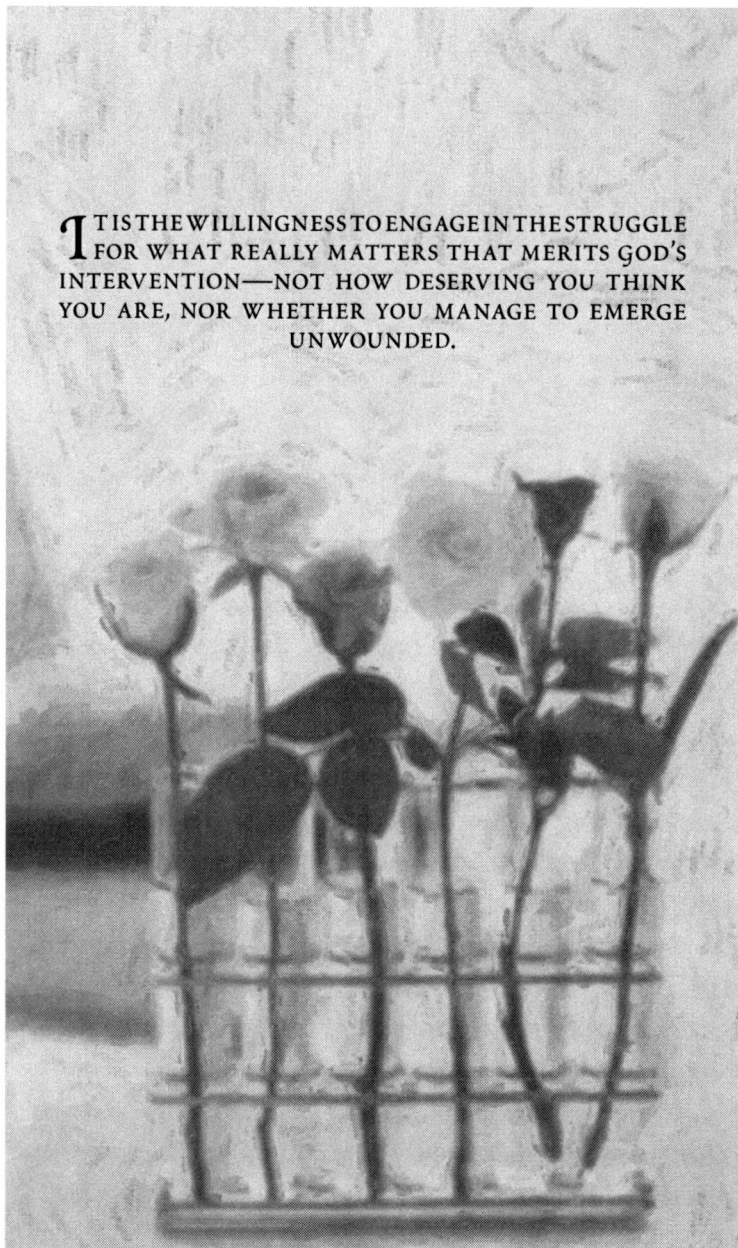

14

Emboldened by the story of Jacob, a thought began forming in my mind so subtle, I'd almost missed it: *Life is about to get interesting again!*

It wasn't only Jacob who inspired this wisp of hope in me. As I thought about the Hebrew Scriptures, the New Testament, the Upanishads and holy books from many other spiritual traditions, I began wondering if I hadn't previously been missing the obvious: God apparently likes a really good story. Depending on which chapter of which book you read, it is all about being oppressed, finding faith, acting with courage, being challenged, journeying out of bondage into the Promised Land. Then there are other themes: loving others unconditionally, standing up to injustice, forgiving one's self and others, redemption, and more.

These stories provide templates for our own lives, showing us the way to a life fulfilling its full potential. Who wants to read a tale in which the heroine allows herself to become passively victimized by life's circumstances, refuses to take risks in a vain effort to hold on to the status quo, and settles for misery and mediocrity day after day? There really had to be something more.

This "something more" was, in fact, the meaning-making enterprise which is at the heart of the soul-infused life. Victor Frankl speaks of this in *Man's Search for Meaning*, his seminal book about the Holocaust. The central human question for him was why some survivors held onto their faith in God and a zest for life, despite the horrors they experienced, while others became resigned or bitter. Those who were able to emerge spiritually intact had what boils down to a talent for meaning-making.

I was back in meaning-making mode today, no longer thinking about how much longer I could hang on by my fingernails. Instead, I found myself wondering what kind of a story God wanted my life to be?

15

I quickly sent out a handful of networking emails before I could think about what I was doing, checking my heart to see if it truly had begun beating again. Miraculously, not only was my heart pumping vigorously, but it was thumping out an increasingly dangerous mantra with every steady beat: *I want, I want, I want*. I was turning away from my helplessness and taking matters into my own hands.

I was like the adventurer who, upon climbing a mountain for the first time, finds herself in a situation in which the only escape is a terrifying leap across an abyss. Having had no experience with such a leap in the past, she has no way to assess her ability to survive. But as scholar William James tells the story, hope and confidence are, in and of themselves, assets that can put the adventurer in the best frame of mind to succeed.

48

James writes:

Believe, and you shall be right, for you shall save yourself;
Doubt, and you shall be right, for you shall perish.
The only difference is that to believe
Is greatly to your advantage.

Surrender, it turns out, has nothing to do with resignation. In fact, true surrender looks the bleakest of realities in the eye and says "I meet your challenge and raise you one. Whatever you send my way, my spirit will be greater."

It takes a degree of recklessness to have faith, especially when all the evidence stacks up against you. But because our futures are open and free, many influences contribute to how our lives will unfold over time. Ironically, my ability to hope was itself becoming one of those factors. It might seem small, but I had the sense that my sheer willingness to take action on my own behalf could carry just enough weight to make the difference.

Affirmation was immediate.

Jason, a top executive from another of the largest global marketing firms, responded by return email to my first brave attempt at online prospecting. He wanted to sit down with me next time he was going to be in L.A. His firm had a job possibility that he wanted to try out on me.

BECAUSE OUR FUTURES ARE OPEN AND FREE, MANY INFLUENCES CONTRIBUTE TO HOW OUR LIVES WILL UNFOLD OVER TIME. IRONICALLY, OUR ABILITY TO HOPE BECOMES ONE OF THOSE FACTORS, CARRYING JUST ENOUGH WEIGHT TO MAKE THE DIFFERENCE.

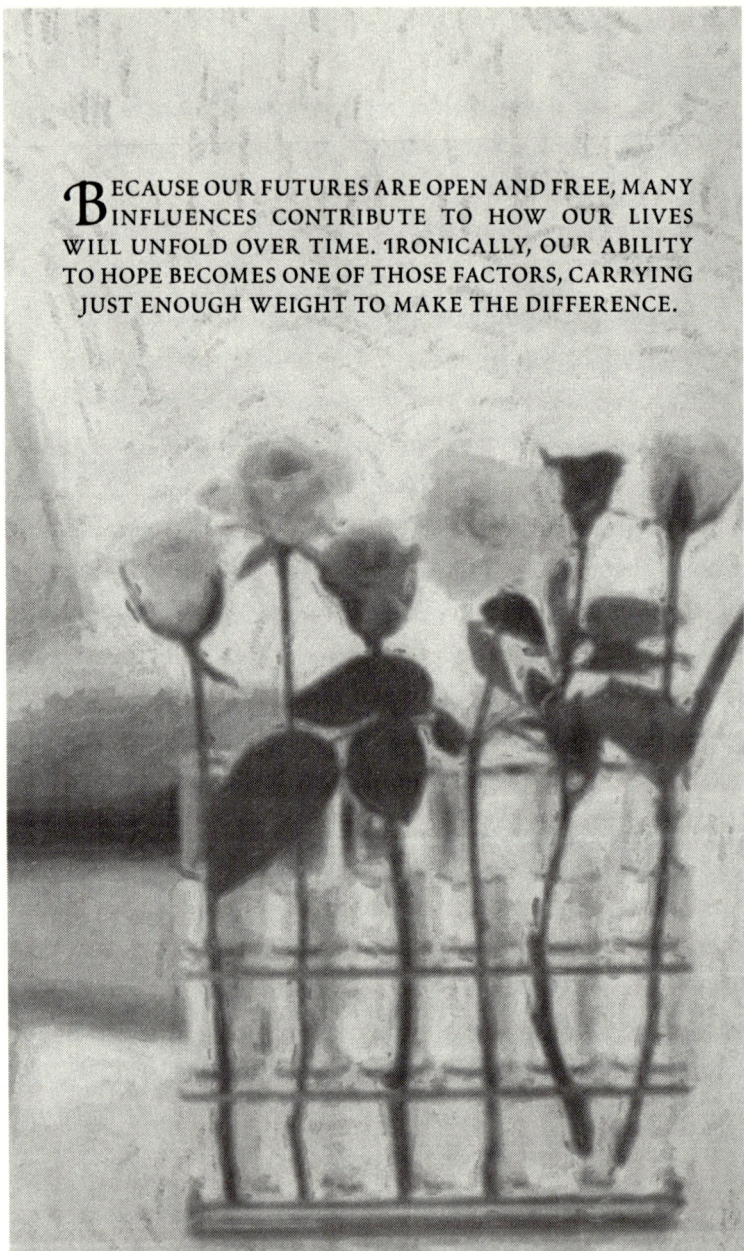

16

Belle was spending more and more time huddled behind closed doors. Meanwhile, desks were suddenly emptying without advance notice. It seemed to those of us who remained that the fluorescent lights had dimmed and the temperature gone frigid. Thank God I had Jason's email in my pocket, even though I had not yet been able to pin down the date for his trip to L.A. In addition, there was always the cracker client as backup. Word was we'd hear any moment now.

It was frankly a relief when I was called away from the office to moderate a panel at a marketing symposium, taking the place of an executive from a competing firm who had suddenly canceled. Rumors were circulating that she'd been let go by her corporation as part of a holding-company-wide staff reduction, but nobody knew for sure.

Wandering the halls and meeting rooms of The 50+ Symposium, I wondered at the brightness of the lights and the warmth of the corridors. In fact, I had suddenly begun feeling like myself again. I was at home in this environment, certain that I would rise to the occasion and that my panel would go well. The very fabric of my being carried the warp and weft of all the speeches I'd given over the years—the panels I'd moderated. My mood rose even higher as I bumped into my peers, friendships made during my travels on the thought leadership circuit. We hugged each other with genuinely enthusiastic hellos.

And then there was a whole series of "good news" emails that I checked on my BlackBerry at breaks. There were several new invitations to join in conference-call brainstormings with executives from our offices around the country. I got a thank-you from one of our offices for research I'd provided. Finally, a press release I wrote to promote our practice had gone out on the wires and was being picked up by numerous media outlets. I was fully aware that the journalists were eager for my opinion not only because of my expertise, but because I was still working for one of the largest and most prestigious marketing firms in the world.

17

Used to work for.
Not long after the ebullient exchange of business cards at the panel's end, I got word. At the end of the month, they were letting me go.

The chairing of the panel at the symposium, all the networking and positioning. Not billable. The new business brainstormings, mentoring and pitches. Not billable. The publication of the press release, the engineering of the research, the interviews with the media. Not billable. Not billable. Not billable. And the cracker account I had hoped would be my salvation? As it turned out, my fate had already been decided, irrelevant of the outcome. The corporate waters had closed over me, silently, relentlessly. Just as easily as Belle and I had been dis-invited from the pitch, I had been rendered invisible.

Over the coming days, there were intermittent communications detailing the ramifications of what Belle had referred to as "my reduction of hours." But all I could do was picture myself, face down on the railroad tracks, seeing the end of employee-paid health coverage rushing inexorably towards me.

18

Long days passed before I could write again. Despite all my brave talk about surrender, I was too deep in the void to find my way to the computer. The one grace I had was that I could still read.

From the depths of her *Journal of Solitude*, poet May Sarton reached out to me:

"In my lifetime, I have seen one comforting myth after another taken apart as I, like everybody else, have tried to come to grips with hard truth…. The marvel is that there are still so many people of courage who go on fighting in spite of all their reasons for despair."

This was not the same void I had written about in my books in the past—the theoretical one in which redemption was possible.

This one was dark and endless, no way out, and now

that I was in it, I was sure that I was the only one in the world who had ever felt this hopeless.

In the inky black, voices whispered to me: *Belle still has her job. Why don't I? If only I'd fought harder to get into that room on that cursed cracker pitch!* And, of course, *What will become of me?*

While I strove to feel God's love embracing me, I was vulnerable to imaginings of the darkest hues.

And the rat didn't help.

19

The rat, unfortunately, was not just my imagination. The rat was real. After calling Dan with the bad news, we had a mournful dinner at a fast-food restaurant and then headed towards the one place I could imagine feeling safe: home, in bed, with the covers pulled over my head.

I will never know if I would have avoided the full-bore void if there hadn't been a rat waiting for us at home. But there was. The evidence was irrefutable: an unopened bag of dog food with a hole chewed into the side and shreds of paper all over the kitchen. It felt like a violation of unbearably rude proportions. We cleaned up, and, exhausted, I slammed shut the bedroom door tight in an act of defiant denial. Just go to sleep. In the morning, things would look brighter.

Then Dan saw it. Closing up the house for the night, he had nearly tripped over the brown blur as it ran from kitchen to living room. Just yesterday, there would have been no question: we would have gone to a hotel and called the exterminator. But we were no longer in a position to shell out real money when gritting our teeth through the night and buying a $5 trap in the morning would do the trick.

Forget the housecleaner and the gardener, while we were at it. And at the end of the month, how could we afford to pay for health care? How long would our savings last? Would we have to rent out rooms to make our payments? And who would rent a room in a house that had a RAT in it?

I'm pretty sure that at least one loving voice, the one who had been coached on and off for years, was trying to get through to me, to remind me that this was unhealthy magical thinking, and that sometimes, a rat is only a rat.

But I knew better. One firing. One rat. Either alone could just be bad luck. But a firing and a rat simultaneously: this was a Message.

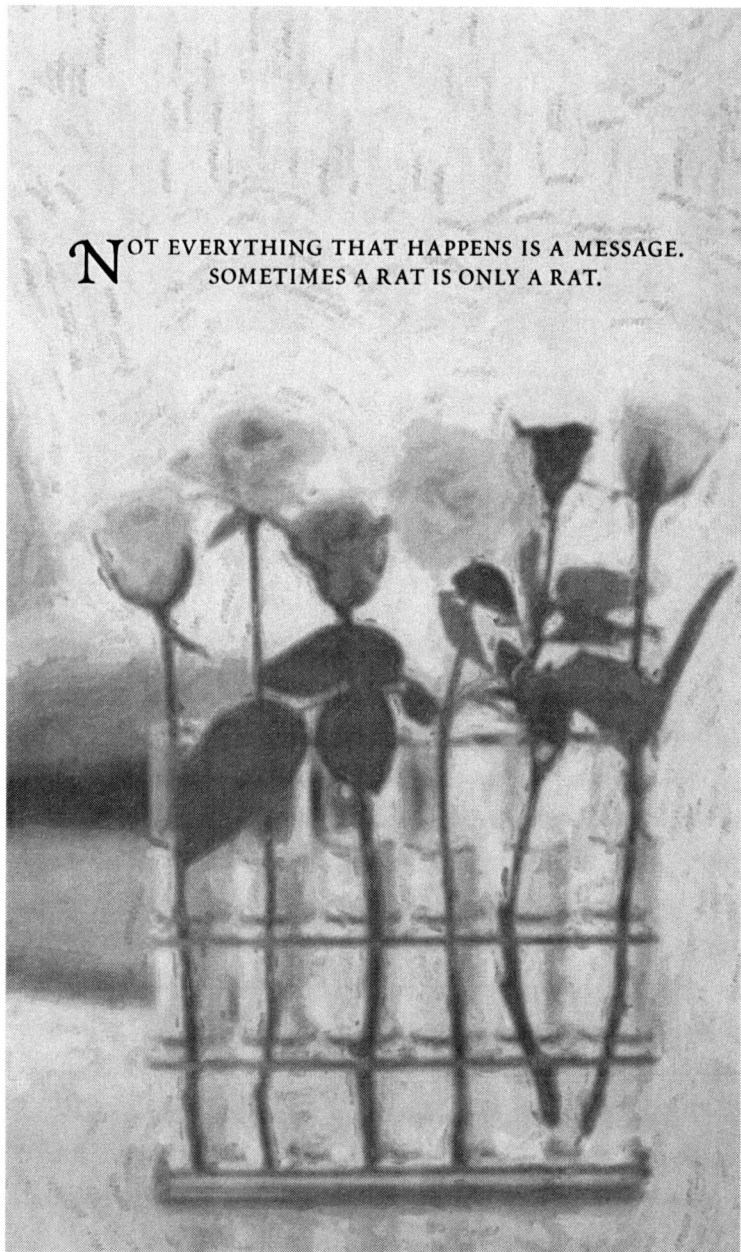

NOT EVERYTHING THAT HAPPENS IS A MESSAGE. SOMETIMES A RAT IS ONLY A RAT.

20

I hate when people quote my own books to me. Not only do I cringe at the gap between whom I aspire to be and who I actually am. It pisses me off.

Dan knew this, but after laying the traps, and plugging the holes and still finding me face down in bed, he knew that for me, this was an emergency. He wanted to read from a book I wrote titled *The Art of Resilience*. I was too limp to resist.

"At the moment of impact, it is natural to focus on your fears. *What's going to happen to me? What else is going to go wrong now? How am I to survive?*

"You think you are being realistic, facing your bleak destiny as if it were cast in stone. But if you are to tell the whole truth, you would have to admit that you don't control the future, any more than you controlled the past.

60

"Just because this disappointment has happened in your life doesn't mean that you won't yet end up with a future far greater than what the past indicates is probable for you. Even as you stand in the shadow of your painful disappointment, if you are honest, you will have to admit that it is just as likely that the best possible outcome will transpire as the worst.

"Always be prepared for anything—but expect only the best."

I tried. I really did. But the truth was, all I was really doing was listening through the words for sounds of fast little feet skittering about on the other side of the door.

21

I would have liked to believe there was something heroic about how I handled getting fired. I'd like to think I was Jacob wrestling at the Jabbok, or the Samurai falling on his sword. In *La Queste del Sainte Graal,* Joseph Campbell tells the story of King Arthur's quest for the Holy Grail. King Arthur's knights are seated at his table, but Arthur will not let the meal be served until an adventure occurs. Sure enough, the Grail appears to them, carried by angelic powers, veiled by cloth. Then it vanishes. Arthur's nephew Gawain proposes that the knights pursue the Grail in order to see it unveiled. And off they go.

Campbell's favorite lines are these: "They thought it would be a disgrace to go forth in a group. Each entered the forest that he had chosen where there was no path and where it was darkest.

"Now, if there's a way or a path, it's someone else's way.... What is unknown is the fulfillment of your own unique life, the likes of which has never existed on the earth. And you are the only one who can do it. People can give you clues how to fall down and how to stand up, but when to fall and when to stand, and when you are falling, and when you are standing, only you can know."

But there was nothing brave or noble about how I was dealing with the blow, nothing spiritual about the rat. I was back wallowing in my self-doubts and fears, repeating yet again that the timing of the rat's appearance in our home was proof that I was useless—even though the holes we plugged now seemed to be holding.

No, I was no Samurai, no King Arthur, no Jacob, not even a lump of coal with the potential to be something more. Rather, I was the woman in the 12-Step tradition story who had been taking a walk on a high mountain path. The woman slipped and fell over the side. Frantically grabbing an overhanging branch, she was dangling a hundred feet above the valley floor when suddenly the branch began to crack.

This woman cried out for help.

"God, are you up there?"

"Yes, my daughter," God replied. "What can I do for you?"

"God, help me. Tell me what to do!" she cried.

"You really want to know?"

The branch cracked a bit more. Desperate, she cried out again.

"Yes, God. Tell me! I'll do whatever you say."

There was a moment's silence. Then God replied:

"Let go of the branch."

"Let go of the branch?"

"Yes, my daughter. Let go of the branch."

There was another moment's silence. Then the woman asked:

"Is there anybody else up there?"

22

Into the void, Human Resources tossed an email that sounded like scolding but was actually an accounting of vacation days left on the books. They were set to *expire* at month's end should I *fail* to use them. Faced with the prospect of the long list of people I should be telling I was fired, but instead sitting for long hours before the computer screen unable to motivate my fingers to punch a single key, this was a spiritual emergency.

Fortunately, an invitation to an art and meditation retreat also found its way into the void. I had been invited by the leader Elena, an artist whose idyllic paintings grace many of our walls with sunny kitchens, forest paths, and happy garden scenes. That said, after twenty years painting pastel settings, she had saturated her market. "We live so damn long," my dear friend had said to me the last time we'd gotten together for lunch. "I've run out of landscapes." The recession didn't help matters any; nor did it help that Elena had failed to pay attention to her cash-flow, using credit cards to bridge the gap. Now she was having trouble even meeting her minimum payments. In fact, she had been on the verge of applying for a shift at her neighborhood Starbucks when she discovered the recession's impact on her potential employer: a "for lease" sign on the green and white front door.

I knew that under these circumstances, Elena was perhaps not the best choice for a spiritual guide. But the date was free and I was desperate. How great it would be to be in a room full of women, all drawn to a spiritual retreat, a special breed, indeed, to be able to simultaneously entertain both questions of survival and the meaning of life. God knows, Elena would have compassion for my situation. This would be a group with whom I could really talk things through. There would, of course, be sage advice. Compassion. Feelings vented. Processing.

I arrived full of hope and let out a hoot of delight when I spied Elena, who promptly put her finger to her lips.

I hadn't read the fine print.

This was a silent retreat.

23

I took my place in the circle of twenty chairs, and sized up the group. Some were wearing colorful peasant gowns, some Chico's and bling, some yoga clothes, and then there I was, in jeans topped by a Burberry suit jacket, having invested in business rather than personal garb during the glory years of my corporate life. We sat quietly in the circle, eyes fixed on a candle flame in the center, contemplating.

Caught somewhere between the spokes of high corporate gear and survival mode, I found the prospect of keeping my mouth shut, let alone quieting my thoughts, daunting. Rather than strangle either into submission, I turned them towards more positive ends. While distracting birds cawed out the window, I closed my eyes and occasionally tuned into what was hacking around in my

own mind. If it was hopeful, I let it be. If it was unpleasant,
which was more often the case, I simply opened my eyes
and thought about how soon until I could get up and eat the
trail mix.

Somehow, the long morning passed and I finally got my
handful of nuts and yogurt chips. But this, too, had to be
consumed in silence.

Then, finally, meditation complete, we moved onto the
second half of the retreat. Elena laid out paint supplies and
a small canvas for each of us. Since there were no words,
I could only surmise that we were to pour the souls we'd
hoped to have encountered in the depths of our individual
silences onto the canvas. I planned to use only those colors
from the palette that truly drew me to them. Follow, don't
lead, I told myself. There were 24 choices, from midnight
blue to cherry red. Instinctively, I went for a bright yellow,
the color of deli mustard. I painted a small circle of the
chosen yellow which I then spiraled outwards, watching
the warm glow grow in concentric circles, overlapping one
another. My brush dried, so I dipped again. Back to the
canvas, again to draw overlapping concentric circles. It was
satisfying, to dip and to brush. I would have liked to have
kept going.

But the canvas was not very big, and while the woman
to the right of me painstakingly started applying green paint
to the first leaf of a bouquet she had outlined in pencil, I
was done. I'd painted the entire stretched square of canvas
solid yellow, and this was only five minutes into the two
hours set aside for this enterprise. Really, I was done.

I pushed away from the table and the stir attracted more

attention than I'd intended. Looks of concern passed over their faces as they started silently slapping at their chests and thighs. Finally, Elena broke the silence. "Wash it out fast. It stains." I looked down at myself, and realized that both the pockets of my Burberry jacket and the front of my designer jeans were covered in yellow paint.

At least I now knew what I would be doing to fill in the next hour and 55 minutes. In the bathroom, I stripped off my clothes and began scrubbing, thinking ruefully that this was as good a use for my talent and skills as anything. And then, I cried. Big, rolling gasps of pain, even as I continued to scrub. And after I washed out as much yellow paint as I could, I caught a glimpse of myself as I stood before the mirror, stripped to my skivvies. Even as tears continued to roll down my cheeks, I realized that I looked truly ridiculous. In fact, mixed in with the sobs were the beginnings of laughter, starting slow like brown water out of rusty pipes, then becoming clearer, gaining strength just as life resumed coursing through my veins.

24

Of course, recovering from the loss of my job, picking up the pieces, and moving on again was, by its very nature, a risky business. But clearly, I had no choice but to submit my fondest notions about how the world works to scrutiny. I was being summoned to heed the call that urged me beyond that which, like it or lump it, no longer served me, and into the unexplored terrain of uncharted territory.

By retreat's end, having laughed and cried, I felt cleansed. The job loss had steamed away like a storm-tossed vessel on a sea of yellow paint and I found myself standing, humbled but hopeful, on the once distant shore of what was to be my new life. I left knowing only the one name I knew before I came, Elena's. But at retreat's end, there was love in that room as tangible as the duck in the retreat center pond. As we hugged goodbye, I knew that this place of loving embrace was as real as Kansas or Iowa. This place would always be there, waiting for me to remember what really matters.

This realization was a good start—but only a start. If Jason wouldn't pin down a date, I would have to resume my job search in earnest. Even more daunting, I would have to find the way to sustain hope during the challenging times ahead when, with the arrival of each credit card bill and mortgage payment, both the financial and spiritual stakes were being raised.

25

When it came to spiritual practice, I imagined something along the lines of heading out every afternoon to do t'ai chi in a city park, or spending a couple of days in private contemplation at the retreat center. In fact, I picked up a brochure at the end of Elena's gathering announcing the availability of inexpensive rooms at the center for individual retreats. I tucked it into my purse: a place of refuge in case I was ever desperate enough to make the call.

But the truth was that having used up the one vacation day I could spare for spiritual emergencies, every other moment was filling rapidly with time spent on hold trying to get past recorded messages as I fit in as many medical services as possible before the employer-paid insurance gave out. In addition, there were lists of people, job websites, friends of friends, headhunters, new possibilities to be organized. How could I possibly find a spiritual practice that could fit around the jagged edges of my erratic schedule?

Then I remembered the *I Ching*. The ancient Chinese book of divination and wisdom had always been there for me when I needed it, a ready source of guidance that had served me for the past forty years. A dorm mate had given me the book shortly after the student health center had tendered me a diagnosis of mononucleosis, a low-grade fever that sapped my energy. The illness left me lying exhausted on a cot in my little room as the world of my childhood came unhinged. Despite the physical misery I was in, I was unwilling to admit defeat by calling home for rescue.

The book with the yellow cover had beckoned to me and I opened at random and began reading through my fever. For days and then weeks, I kept turning to new pages, often having not the foggiest idea how to interpret the poetic and cryptic phrases. When something did speak to me, I often found it more challenging than comforting. But eventually, the *I Ching*'s words, once cryptic, began delivering cogent, insightful advice.

Over three thousand years ago, leaders marshaled their forces and marched into battles to fight for issues they deeply believed in. They didn't always win. Sometimes it was character traits that did them in—arrogance or impatience. Sometimes it was immutable fate. Sometimes they decided that the wisest course was not to fight at all, or to find the perfect moment to retreat. They recovered to try again—or they transcended the mainstream of everyday life to develop themselves further.

Finding myself in the *I Ching*'s pages, I eventually made it through the illness and continued on with my studies and my life.

The I Ching had helped me through the thicket of life's often confusing challenges many times over since then. Could *The I Ching* help me now? I knew exactly where to find it, discovering—as I suspected—that it was covered with dust. I pulled it from the shelf and began to read.

26

*T*he *I Ching* teaches that there are multiple models of success. In the paradigm we've adopted in the West, we are taught at an early age that progress is a vertical climb from obscurity to success. The ascent should be flawless. Every life event should represent a brisk stride forward. All you need to do is to work hard, be smart, and keep your eyes focused on what you want. If you have to push through your fears and feelings, you do so. If you have to set aside your values or ignore the urge to nurture yourself or others, so be it.

There is a problem with this model, however, for when you commit yourself to letting nothing get in your way, you become brittle and reactive. You set yourself against the universe, inadvertently increasing resistance to your efforts by the nature of your rigid stance.

Wouldn't it be better if there were a model of success that didn't view pain and setback as an aberration, but rather as a healthy part of a successful life process? The *I Ching* presents an alternative, basing its wisdom on the cycles of nature.

The ancient Chinese noticed that everything in nature is in a constant state of change. Just when a season or stage reaches its peak, it inevitably turns into its opposite. Fall dies to winter, preparing the soil for the rebirth of spring. Summer fades into the fall, starting the cycle over and over again. Living creatures are born, mature, give birth, age, and die. From the rich soil of their graves sprout seeds of new life.

The *I Ching* teaches that you cannot judge the truth of the seasons by staying only on the surface. You must live many years, gain the perspective of many seasons, to be able to comprehend the real work that is taking place at any given time.

So it was in my life. It may have looked to others that winter had bared my branches. But neither I nor anybody else could truly judge what was really going on with me by looking only at my external manifestations. For beneath the bark, what was really happening was that the sap was starting to flow, new life was being created long before it became visible as leaves and fruit. In nature, destruction is often the prerequisite for new growth, like the bursting open of a jack pine cone in the heat of a forest fire, releasing its seeds to the soil.

The *I Ching* teaches us that when you are fully alive, you are continually asked to let go of what you have in order to make space for new possibilities to come to you. You free your essential spirit from the need to protect what you have already achieved, and relax into an expanded vision of fulfilling your true potential. There is growth. There is progress. However, this is advancement not despite your challenges, but including them.

It is progress, then, to give up the rigid stance that proclaims that you will succeed, allowing nothing to get in your way. Rather, you embrace the possibility that many things are bound to get in your way. Success comes not in spite of the things that happen to you—the good and the bad—but because you have grown large enough to embrace it all.

EMBRACE THE POSSIBILITY THAT MANY THINGS ARE BOUND TO GET IN YOUR WAY. SUCCESS COMES NOT IN SPITE OF THE THINGS THAT HAPPEN TO YOU BUT BECAUSE YOU HAVE GROWN LARGE ENOUGH TO EMBRACE IT ALL.

27

Inspired by the *I Ching*, I was finally able to send another flurry of emails to my list. More than a half-dozen bounced back, several informing me that the intended recipient was no longer with the firm. There were a few "nothings now" and some "I will keep my eyes open for you."

But it didn't all come up empty, for mixed into the emails was a message from Jason. He was getting closer to setting the dates for his trip to L.A. and wanted to find a time to speak by phone about the job first. He didn't want to wait any longer.

This was a hopeful sign, indeed. In fact, this felt no less than salvation.

At the appointed hour of our phone date, I lit a scented candle, put Lucky in the bedroom lest she begin to bark, and stared at the phone, willing it to ring.

Later, after I emailed Jason to ask if I'd somehow gotten the time wrong, he emailed back that there had been an emergency.

I forgave him—but then again, I was desperate to believe in something. Frankly, the job-hunting process was not going well. Aside from the instantaneous bounce backs, the pace was still very slow. Emails took days, not hours, to elicit a response, if any. When I did hear back, more often than not it was only to hear "there's nothing new."

28

I was disappointed that after Jason's original, fast response, I was having trouble pinning down the date for the phone call, let alone the meeting in L.A. The fact was, Jason's job was my only hope, as I had now contacted everybody I could possibly think of. I even posted my resume on various online websites and checked every help wanted I could find.

Nothing. Nada. Nix.

I began to consider the possibility that going into the void was not a temporary condition from which I could escape. I had, it seemed, taken up permanent residence. That said, I knew from my spiritual studies that this was not necessarily a bad thing. Most religions have the equivalent of the void. In Christianity, it's the Dark Night of the Soul. In Zen, it's Emptiness.

What could possibly be spiritual about Nothing? Because, we are taught, it is in the void that the status quo has the lightest hold on us. Released from the constructs of our everyday life, we have the least to lose. In the void, we are free to make substantive changes in our lives.

By this theory, without my knowing it, I had actually quietly been making spiritual progress, even when I was feeling cynical, angry, despondent, abandoned, and resentful. In fact, through the texts of many faith traditions, we learn that it is often the unlikeliest amongst us who are candidates for the inbreaking of spirit. A shepherd stutters on a mountaintop in the presence of God. A beggar woman's hand shakes as she reaches out to touch a sacred hem. A supplicant, feeling lowlier than a worm, prostrates himself at the foot of his guru.

As Rabbi Abraham Joshua Heschel once wrote, the way to face the light is to come full of fear and trembling at our presumption for being as flawed as we are, humbled through our disappointments and personal failings, yet still having the audacity to believe in the possibility of an encounter with the divine.

IT IS IN THE VOID THAT THE STATUS QUO HAS THE LIGHTEST HOLD ON US. RELEASED FROM THE CONSTRUCTS OF OUR EVERYDAY LIFE, WE HAVE THE LEAST TO LOSE. IN THE VOID, WE ARE FREEST TO MAKE CHANGES.

29

I say that it was in retrospect that I was making spiritual progress because there was nothing wondrous at the time about feeling like a worm. It was a blessing that fate, however, did not seem to care what mood I was in, optimistic or despairing, courageous or fearful. The truth was that I really was not in control. There were forces at work in my life far greater than my moods and emotions. I could not be good enough, work hard enough, be deserving enough, or think positively enough to ensure that I would get things to turn out the way I thought I deserved. Even if I did everything I could to hold onto a positive attitude, I could well be strung out longer in my job hunt than I'd ever anticipated. But the flip side was also dawning on me: I could be depressed and get an offer for a job five minutes from now. The good news was that I didn't need an upbeat or even brave attitude to make progress. I just needed discipline, putting resumes out, making phone calls, following up leads. This I could do happy or sad, anxious or full of faith.

Although it had come in fits and starts, my outreach had slowly begun paying off. While I was still on hold with Jason, my inbox was stirring with signs of life. Here was a heartfelt message, empathetic curiosity, the name of someone to contact. Here was an offer to pass along my resume and the email addresses of a top headhunter.

So why after a genuine "thank you!" to each and every one, was I putting off following up on their suggestions?

I didn't like the answer, even then. But the truth was, I was still waiting for Jason. Clearly, his was the job that God had designated for me—the only ready-made option that had emerged from the ethers that held the promise of restoring my full salary, benefits, and position. As soon as Jason and I connected, I was certain I would be granted a free pass around the messiness and rejection of the job-hunting process, stop slipping down the prestige and job security pole, and shoot right back up to the top.

But there was something else. I was also still a worm. And what I wanted more than anything in the world was someone to take care of me. I wanted my company to lift the banishment, Jason to adopt me, anybody to save me. In fact, if I could have thought of a way to make any of this happen, I would have grabbed it. But I couldn't.

YOU DON'T NEED AN UPBEAT OR EVEN A BRAVE ATTITUDE TO MAKE PROGRESS. YOU JUST NEED DISCIPLINE, PUTTING RESUMES OUT, MAKING PHONE CALLS, FOLLOWING UP LEADS AND THE LIKE. THIS YOU CAN DO HAPPY OR SAD, ANXIOUS OR FULL OF FAITH.

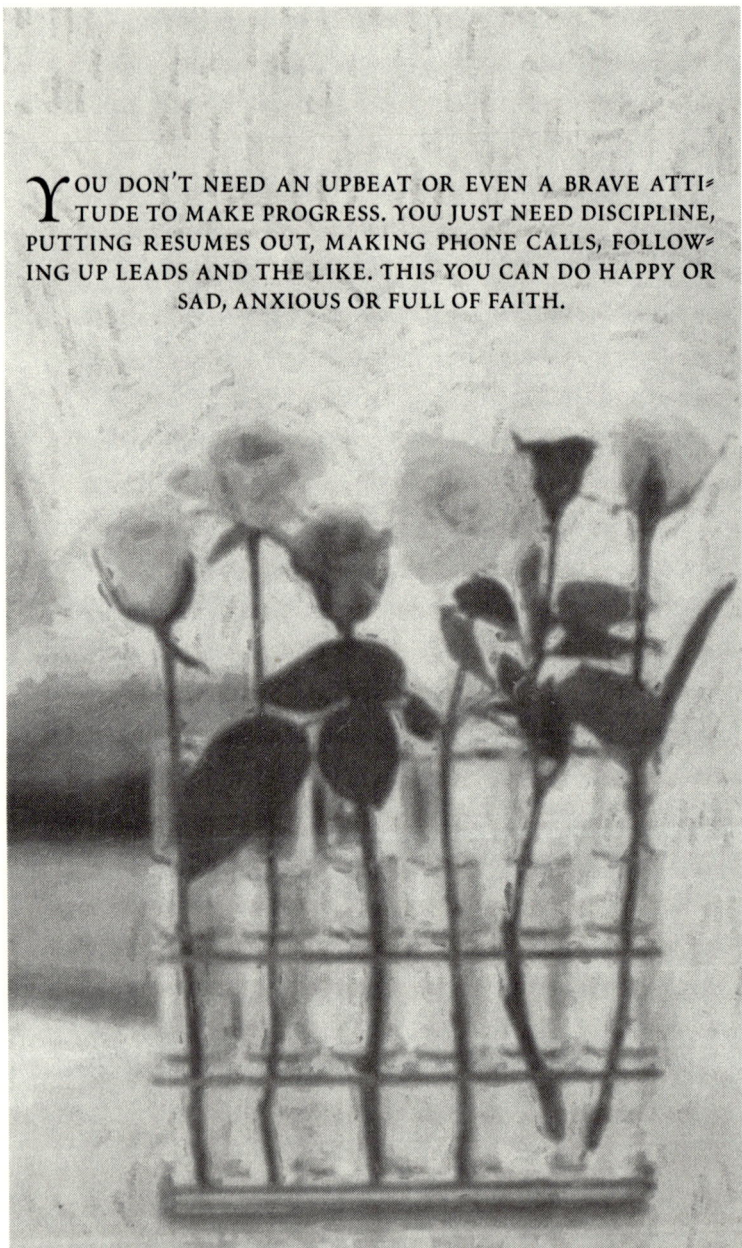

30

As the days rolled, with no further calls or emails from Jason, I was now at full stop, ordered back to Joan's office by Dan, who trusted that she would once again breathe life into my dry bones. So there I was, telling her for the third time in twenty minutes how critical and inevitable it was that Jason would offer me the job and at the same time, how long I was spending staring helplessly at the phone and email screen waiting to hear from him. Then I made the mistake of mentioning the emails from others that had begun filling my inbox with offers to help.

Joan seized the opportunity. In short order, I felt like the witness to a train wreck in progress, ducking for cover as unexpected words came flying out of her mouth like dangerous debris off the track. Words like "business cards," "website," "announcement."

By the time I hit the elevator to the garage, I was morose. Joan had told me to stop waiting for Jason and start a new company of my own. "You've done it before. You can take charge of your own destiny. Be your own boss." She asked me to think of this as an opportunity for reinvention—that I was ready to shed my corporate skin and move forward into something more closely aligned with my mission.

"Perhaps this was the deeper meaning and purpose of this period of your life—the opportunity to come even closer to a merger between making a living and fulfilling your purpose."

Of course there was risk in going this route. I knew all about the pressures of starting and running one's own enterprise, especially in a rotten economy. That was why I had set my company aside in the first place and gone for my doctorate. I had burned out on making payroll, occasionally forced to issue pink slips of my own. But Joan pressed on. "It's time to stop asking who wants you and place your attention on what it is that you have to offer. Where is the convergence between your skills, abilities, and knowledge and that for which others would be willing to pay? Who is in a position to value what you have and the world needs?"

I wanted to humor her by saying I agreed that I should start my own company, but it was images of Jason and the multinational corporation he represented that illuminated my job horizon: a glowing orb of power, privilege, and security that blotted out all else.

Clearly, I was not ready to start my own business, to take on those risks and responsibilities. Nor would I need to. Hadn't she heard me say loud and clear that Jason had a real job he wanted to talk to me about? Joan had for the first time misfired. Why hadn't she seen how far off the mark she'd been?

31

Just as the elevator at Joan's office building reached the basement garage, my cell phone rang. It was Jason's secretary on the line. Jason was in L.A. and would like to see me at a restaurant near their downtown office in an hour. Could I make it?

The timing was divine, a vindication of my refusal to give up on Jason's job. If God wasn't behind this job offer, why was this the one opportunity that had manifested for me?

I was reminded of a story Elena once shared with me. A woman's house was in the path of a flood. She crawled up to her roof and started to pray.

"God save me!"

She was so firm in her faith that she was absolutely certain that God would carry her to safety. And so, when a helicopter flew overhead, she waved it on. Then a boat came by and she passed up the invitation to board. Eventually, the water was over her head and she drowned. At last, she was face to face with God in heaven.

"God, why didn't you save me?" she cried out to God. "Where were you when I needed you?"

God replied, "I flew over you in a helicopter, but you waved me on. I steered the boat up to you, but you refused to board."

I understood this woman, but I'd learned over the years to recognize God in unexpected places and circumstances. No matter how strongly Joan was advocating for me to start my own business, my belief remained unshaken: Jason's job was the helicopter that showed up, the boat that arrived, the door that finally opened.

Snatched from the void, I pointed the nose of my Saturn towards the high-rises in the center of town. Jason and I were to have lunch at a trendy place and joining us was to be the head of the L.A. office, Wendy. Vaguely, I wondered why she'd been invited. Certainly Jason was considering me for a global position. What did Wendy, a regional manager, have to do with anything?

32

There were no last-minute cancellations. There I was at last, at the appointed destination. The young hostess led me through the restaurant to a glass and chrome booth. I hadn't been in an expensive restaurant since I'd been fired, and I looked at the diners in fancy suits and Prada—still employed—as if they were denizens of another planet. Jason, master of this universe, held the key.

When I arrived, Wendy and Jason were seated across from one another each hunched over their BlackBerries. The only sound was the insistent beat of urban hip hop over the Muzak system and the muted clicking of keys. I greeted them, and Wendy looked up and smiled while Jason merely talked while continuing to type. "I'm in the middle of a crisis," he said loudly, over the music. "I'll be with you shortly."

I had plenty of time to observe Jason unnoticed, as the crisis did not resolve even as we ordered drinks, read the menu, chose our entrees, and had them served. Jason, in black-on-black business casual, wore a bald head as if it were the trendiest of accessories. Wendy, also in black but topped by colorful glasses and a shaggy hairdo, would have fit in seamlessly with the team who had frozen me out of the cracker account. In this firm, Jason was obviously the grownup and Wendy the next generation of leadership.

After Wendy and I completed the preliminary small talk, Jason was still in crisis mode. Without a moment's hesitation, Wendy launched into the formal interview.

"What clients were you handling? What were your billings? Was leaving your position your choice?" Hadn't she read the headlines, revealing the company's layoffs?

I looked over to Jason, to see if he were at least eavesdropping. But no, he was tapping away. Had I misunderstood? Was this, indeed, a regional position, reporting to Wendy?

There were limits, even for the desperate job-seeker. This was one of them.

"Jason," I cleared my throat. "I'm not sure if I have your attention, and I'm assuming these are responses you'll need to hear. I'd hate to have to say everything twice."

"You're so right, Carol. I'm being rude. Please, go on and enjoy your meal and I'll be right back."

With that, Jason got up from the table and strode out of the restaurant, tapping as he walked.

33

Somewhere, birds were chirping. A fat, plucky duck dipped her bill into the water and waved her little orange feet in the air. And the reason I knew this was because I was seated on a bench at the retreat center where I'd not long ago covered myself in yellow paint, looking at them.

To make a long story short, Jason came back just after Wendy and I completed dessert. I had given in and (is there no shame?) did the interview with her. She continued to press for details about client billings, sounding a lot like Belle. Of course, I only offered up generalities. She was equally vague, so I still had no idea regarding the role for which I was being recruited. But I was beginning to fear the worst.

The moment Jason was seated—profuse apologies—

94

Wendy excused herself for another meeting. Then (is there truly no end to my shame?) I did the interview again with him. At least this time, crisis resolved, I had his full attention.

Despite myself, I found him to be smart, funny, empathetic, competent and inspiring, even as he speedily chomped his way through his meal while I nursed my last bites. By the time he caught up to me, we were actually jamming.

"Marketers are catching on to this Boomer thing," said Jason. "But brand marketing is just part of the picture. There's the internal communications component, as well."

"Yes: the workplace. And not just Boomers—intergenerational relations." I replied.

"And not just intergenerational relations, but retention and recruitment of seasoned workers, mentoring and succession issues, not despite but because of our recessionary times!"

"Allowing corporations to make better use of human resources, reducing turnover, and saving on costly mistakes and retraining!" As I recreate the dialogue, sitting on my bench overlooking the pond, I'm not even sure which words were coming out of whose mouth.

To the outside observer, Jason and I sat kitty-corner from one another at the lunch table. But, in truth, we both stood like a pair of skilled jugglers tossing hopes and aspirations back and forth between us on the corporate interview stage. Masterful, electric: I lobbed my capabilities, insights and experiences to Jason who caught them as dazzling plates and saucers and twirled them on his arms, legs and even the tip of his BlackBerry before throwing them gracefully back to me where I spun them on my head. "This could work," I know he was thinking, because I was thinking it too. A spinning platter of corporate support here, a global swat team of peers twirling there, potential business needing to be reeled in hurtling through the air, a masterful catch culminating in his final leaping pronouncement:

"Organizational communications: Something companies even need in a bad economy—heck, need especially in a bad economy. And a place you'd fit."

We were one.

But there was a catch.

Now, as I sat on my bench, the fat white duck floated serenely by. From the placid look of her, you'd never guess how hard those little orange feet were paddling.

"This would be a no-brainer if you could bring in a client with you. If you have something in, say, the million-dollar-plus range, we could kick it upstairs."

All at once, the saucers, the plates, every manner of twirling thing crashed to the floor and broke into little bits. Then his BlackBerry kicked back in and we were hurrying out of the restaurant.

"Why don't you sleep on it?" he was saying as he ran for a cab, scampering away into the distance and out of sight.

34

So there I was, sitting by the pond watching the ducks and butterflies. After lunch, I'd crawled back home just long enough to call the number on the brochure I'd been carrying with me since Elena's gathering, finding out that there was, indeed, one room available for a few days' individual retreat. I grabbed a change of clothes, hugged Dan goodbye, and fled seeking refuge. I was definitively back in the void, realizing how foolish I'd been to pin all my hopes on Jason, desperate for salvation.

Back in the void. No coach. No art workshop. No advice from anybody. I just sat and administered to myself a sober assessment of the state of my soul. As desperate as I was for Jason's job, I would not have taken a client with me from my former employer, even if there were one that would have come with me. But perhaps there was a lesson in all this for me—something important that, painful as all this was, constituted some kind of wedge of growth. The loss of my job and my failure to get snapped up quickly was clearly a message, telling me that it was time to toughen up. Next time, it would be incumbent upon me to do everything within my power to ensure that I would be the last one standing, not the one who ended up with the wobbly chair and the pink slip. To be spiritual—but to find the courage to stand solidly in my center of power. This was where the growth was. After all, even I had the right to make a living, utilize my gifts fully, and exercise the authority I'd worked so hard and long to earn. I deserved to be honored for my years of experience, my wisdom, and my hard work.

This was true for me, and for all Boomer women. It's a sacred duty to take the risk of speaking up for ourselves more honestly and more often. If Jason's job wasn't real, surely there would be another where I would use my positional power to get people to perform their roles and tasks, without apologizing, defending, begging, or demeaning myself in any way. I would summon the courage to tell others when they've messed up, holding them accountable.

This was the meaning of this job loss, the meaning for which I'd been searching: the salvation of my fully-integrated soul that would shout out to one and all: "This is me. Deal with it."

35

The point of a spiritual retreat is to disengage from the outside world. This certainly covers not making surreptitious phone calls to one's spouse while huddling behind a boulder at the far end of the duck pond. But I had to make just one call.

Dan didn't answer. Leaving a voice mail was not the way I'd hoped to deliver this critical message, but it couldn't wait.

"Dan. I'm not done yet! Even if Jason's job isn't going to work out, another corporate job will. I have been set free to claim the culmination of all my life's work—a chance to play an even bigger role on the world stage. I've learned so much about myself and I really want to have the opportunity to test it out in the largest arena possible."

As soon as I left the message for Dan, an unbidden thought washed away my certainty. Of course, who wouldn't benefit from toughening up, speaking your mind more freely and owning your power? But then again, doesn't there come a time in your life when you have done enough self-improvement? And when that moment arrives, doesn't the better question become *What is it that this already good-enough person wants?*

The answer was obvious. I would not want to put myself in an environment where I would have to steel myself daily just to show up and then have to worry all over again about being laid off. In any case, there weren't any corporations hiring in my field, for just about any job at all, let alone thought leadership.

But what was the alternative? As Joan said, to start my own consulting practice?

This was a demanding path that would require me to invest in myself. I'd have to take the already eroded stash of money set aside for later in life and use even more of it now. We would have to dip into our savings that were meant to help us fund the extra years our generation was predicted to live.

But then again, if biology had determined to give our generation a longevity bonus of thirty or forty more years of life, then in the true scope of things, I was young, indeed. With three or four decades more, if I had to whittle away at our retirement funds to start my company, there would be plenty of time to make the money back. If, on the other hand, I died earlier than anticipated, it wouldn't have made any difference, anyway.

Invest in myself and start my own business?

Once again, I ducked behind the boulder. I just had to

make one more call.

"Dan" I spoke into the answering machine. "I've just realized what a fool I've been. Of course, it should have been obvious all along. Joan was so right. I'm meant to start my own company. I don't need to build a big staff. I can just do something simple, virtual, online. Even so, I know it will be challenging—but I also know this is what I'm meant to be doing...what this has all been about. So could you do me a big favor? Look in my desk drawer and pull out the template for my old business consulting cards. I'm pretty sure the contact numbers are still good. Anyway, could you drop it by Kinko's and get some cards printed? I want to get a running start at this as soon as I get home!"

36

So why was I crying?

I'd completed silent breakfast in the refectory followed by a stroll down to the pond. I'd brought my journal with me, intending to analyze the dream I'd wakened to in the middle of the night, hoping it would somehow shed some light on why I'd made a decision but still felt terrible. In the dream, I watched helplessly as Lucky fell into a raging river. Dan jumped in after her and the two were swept away. I ran downstream to save them and there was a helicopter—but I couldn't get it to lift off. There was a boat—I couldn't start the engine. When I awoke, my heart still raced, and I lay back on the pillows to take whatever comfort I could in the fact that at the end of the dream, I had still been trying to save them. Maybe there was still hope. Nevertheless, it was a horrible dream.

That was not, however, why I was at the pond sobbing onto my journal, yesterday's ink running down the page and onto my jeans. When I opened my notebook, I saw that I had filled my journal with budgets, names of prospective clients, copy for the web site, and product descriptions. But my tears were melting entire columns of lists and charts as I faced the stark truth: I was scared. Not only was I terrified that I didn't really have it in me to pull this off, but I was afraid that I was mistaken in thinking that this was what I was meant to do.

But I was crying for another reason, too. I was crying because saving my (downsized) soul was turning out to be a serious matter, one that had very little to do with whether I should resume looking for a big corporate job, start my own company, or pursue something I hadn't even considered yet. For unless I had faith, I was lost anyway.

And sitting there on that little bench, I was certain that that was the case.

Once upon a long time ago, I was whole. But life got to me, and now my soul was broken to the core. I was utterly hopeless and absolutely correct in thinking it didn't matter what I did, look for a job or start my own business, or nothing at all, for that matter. I was damaged beyond repair.

All that was left of me was a cry of despair, gushing out the last broken bits in the form of a prayer.

"God, I give up. Do whatever you will with me. I'm done. Amen."

37

I was still crying as I headed back to my little room, thinking nothing could make me cry harder. But in fact, there was something. As I approached the hermitage, I saw that Dan and Lucky were sitting on the front porch, waiting for me. Dan held a beautiful bouquet of flowers. And Lucky was dressed up in a brand new pink bow with a big purple rose made of gauze clipped to the ponytail at the top of her head.

"We missed you," Dan said simply. "And I wanted to bring you your cards."

The business cards—the ones I'd asked Dan to get printed for me. How could I admit to him that I was already no longer sure I wanted to start my own business after all?

"I got raised blue ink" he said, pointing to a long oblong box wrapped in plain brown paper.

I started crying again.

"Thank you so much. But, oh God, this is so embarrassing. I have figured out that I don't have it in me to start my own business. Or land a job with a corporation, or any job for that matter. Or do anything ever again. In fact, it's even too late to save my soul. It's broken—I'm broken—to the core."

There was utter silence. And then Dan started laughing.

"That's the most ridiculous thing I've ever heard," he said.

"I am broken," I repeated, louder this time, "to the core."

"Your soul is just fine," Dan replied. "It's the economy that's broken, not you."

Again, utter silence. And then, to everybody's relief, I started laughing, too.

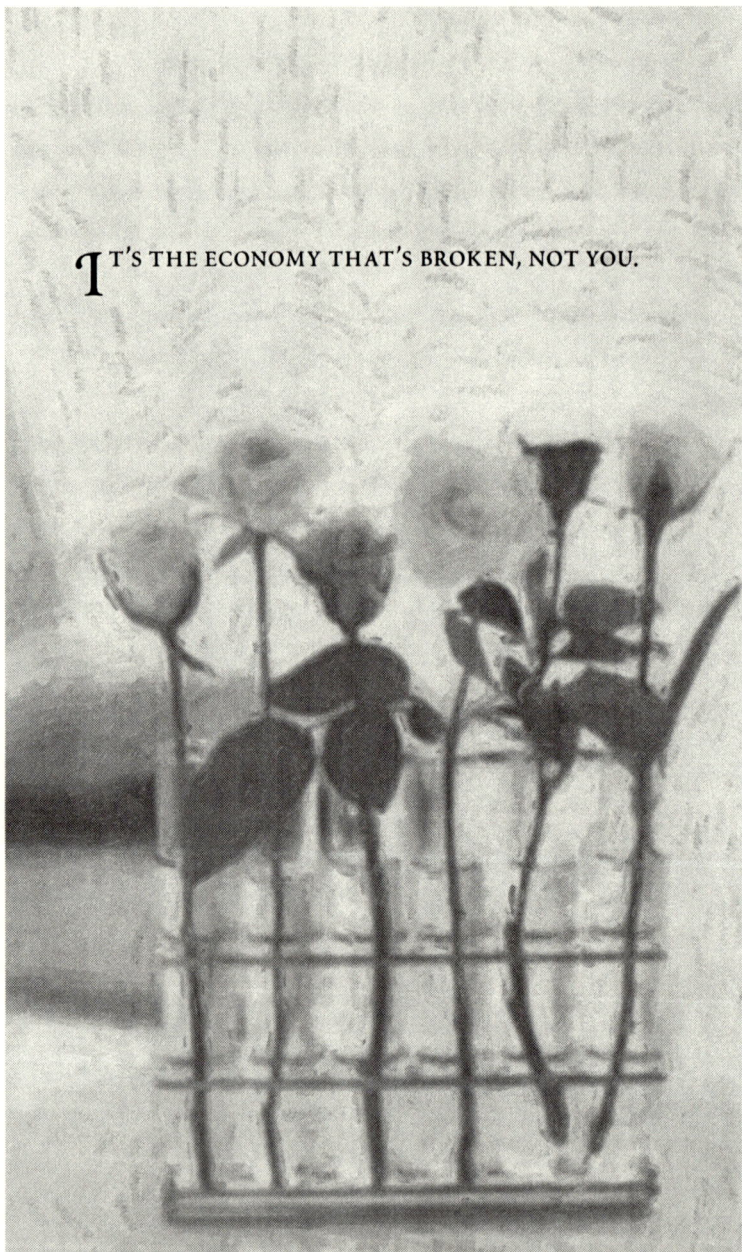

I<small>T'S THE ECONOMY THAT'S BROKEN, NOT YOU.</small>

38

It wasn't until later, long after Dan and Lucky left my little hermitage, that I remembered the box of cards he'd brought. The package sat on the bedside table, beneath the bouquet of flowers. Tomorrow I would have to come home and make some kind of decision about what I would be doing next, and I still didn't have a clue.

As I reached for the box, I recalled Lucky jumping up and down as Dan and I had hugged at the door, thinking that the box of cards held some kind of treat. Suddenly, I was remembering not only this happy moment, but everything that had happened this year: the evening Lucky and I chased the sunset, the wobbly chair, all the emails about return on investment, the rat, yellow paint on my pants, the applause at the end of my panel, my lunch with Jason and Wendy. I remembered my hopes and my aspirations. My naivety and how much I'd learned. The stupid things I'd said and done. The wise things, too.

Then I tore off the brown wrapping paper, opened the lid and pulled out a card. Printed in bold letters, centered on the pure white rectangle in raised dark blue ink, on each one of the thousand cards were the words:

WORLD'S GREATEST
ENTERTAINMENT

39

Instantly, I understood what the cards meant. Dan was letting me know that he had utter faith that regardless of the battering my spirit had endured, the show would go on. It didn't matter to him whether I looked for another corporate job or started my own business—or something else entirely. He knew that once my feet got going, adventures were sure to unfold. There would be tears, laughter, suspense, pathos.

And, too, sooner or later, once again somebody would realize that they need what it is I have to offer and would pay for it, to boot. The box full of cards may just as well have said "You are loved, no matter what" a thousand times over.

The last morning at the retreat center, I wandered over to the library and pulled a book from the shelf. The work was Joan D. Chittister's *Scarred by Struggle, Transformed by Hope.* I serendipitously opened to page 37 and began to read: "It isn't true that the loss of any single thing will destroy us. Everything in life has some value and life is full of valuable things, things worth living for, things worth doing, things worth loving again. It is only a matter of being detached enough from one thing to be open to everything else."

It had taken a whole year of preparation, but I finally got it. The year I had set aside to save my (downsized) soul had not come up empty. I now realized that even the broken bits of my job, career, and life were part of the whole. Even in the worst of it, standing neck-deep in the rubble, something essential in me had endured. This core aspect of myself that sat in witness through everything that transpired, that stuck with me through all manner of betrayal, rejection, and stupidity, that brought discipline and compassion to recording it all dutifully in this record of my year: it was none other than the very soul I'd set out to save. In the end, it was not I who saved my soul. It was my soul that saved me.

40

Some time passed before Elena and I got together again. Out of the blue, she had called to invite me to lunch—and she was offering to pay. Over a nice glass of wine, Elena told me that shortly after the art and meditation retreat, she had taken a booth at a local arts festival. Because of the recession, the fair got off to a slow start, visitors few and far between.

Elena then and there determined to take a seat inside her little tent on a folding chair, surrounded by her art, and vowed not to leave it until she received a message from the universe regarding her new subject matter. "I sat for about an hour undisturbed when a passer-by's Pekinese wandered into my tent and jumped into my lap. I heard its owner calling 'Peaches, Peaches!' I was completely ticked off that my ritual had been spoiled, but I had no choice but to break my vow, leave the tent, and return Peaches to her distraught owner."

After many kisses and licks from her rescued Pekinese, the passer-by looked up from Peaches and uttered four apocryphal words: "Do you paint pets?"

Instantly Elena knew she had her new subject matter. By the time we'd gotten around to setting this lunch date, she was fully booked for sittings with patrons' cats, dogs, and birds.

41

"But what about you?" Elena asked. She really wanted to know how things were turning out.

I caught her up on everything that had happened to me from the day I'd covered myself with yellow paint through opening the box of cards. But by then it was getting late, and Elena had to leave for a sitting with a long-haired dachshund. We hugged, and promised to get together again soon. Then I hurried home, wanting to catch my memoir up to date. So here goes:

For starters, I never heard from Jason again.

Instead, I dug in and began following up on the emails from friends and associates that had previously gone untended. Eventually I landed my first and then my second project. They were small, and I barely noticed that I had moved off of dead stop. But organically, little by little, the wheels of my consulting practice had begun turning. Frankly, I still didn't know if running a business was what I wanted to do, but I knew the time had definitively come for me to do something—it really didn't matter what. If I didn't have a grand plan, at least I could always just do what was next. Even if it was only one baby step at a time, I trusted that, as I took action, forces would be put into motion that would bring new opportunities my way.

Dan and I continued to cut back on expenses, and we did start drawing down on our savings to fund our transition. But anticipating downsizing had proven to be more terrifying than adjusting to our new circumstances. I was, at last, finding out what it was like to live on the other side of fear.

Even those in my network of friends and associates who had no jobs or projects for me were eager to do what they could. For some, that meant sharing the story of their own recession crisis. I discovered that almost everybody who has worked in a company has one, even the most successful of my friends. Many were in various states of transition themselves, and we bonded deeply over long walks. The conversations were warm and bittersweet, as we surveyed our devalued real estate, trying to figure out, only half in jest, who would move into whose guest house if things didn't improve.

42

Over the weeks that ensued, I worked on my two projects and nurtured the stray leads that sprouted from the fertile ground, dutifully tending my little garden of possibilities. Most of the tender green sprouts turned out to be weeds. Of these, some shot up like swamp grass, waving giddily about in the sun for a moment and then were gone by morning.

But one was not a weed—and miraculously, it took root. It sprung out of a seed planted by a friend. She had met someone starting up a dot.com in the social marketing space: a networking site for upscale women 50+. She thought we should talk.

This time, my forwarded email got a fast reply and in less time than it had taken Jason to return a single one of my calls, I was flying to the company headquarters and offered a position.

I landed a job as Senior Strategist with VibrantNation. com. My role: thought leadership. The field: social networking. The mission: getting women over 50 the respect we deserve.

I had inadvertently reinvented myself, and in a field that did not even exist at the beginning of my career, when I'd originally established my aspirations and set my course. As it turns out, this field—this job—had literally been beyond my wildest dreams.

43

I work virtually out of L.A. now, and here's the thing: I'm happy. Of course, I'm both making and spending less. But I like the CEO and the people with whom I work. After the drama and chaos, I have landed in an alternative universe where life makes sense again. And I've learned one final lesson about giving up control. While it's true that you can't always stop bad things from happening, you can't stop good things from happening either.

The truth is that saving one's (downsized) soul does not look pretty. It is certainly not paint-by-numbers on a stretched white canvas. Rather, this most important of all tasks asks something much greater of us: that we become larger than the uncertainties of life, the pain and problems, and trust that it is all ultimately heading towards the good. This is life's promise to us: not that we always get what we think we want, but that we have the capacity to become great enough to embrace it all.

You can get to a place in your life where you no longer obsess about the paint on your pants or the savings in your bank account or the stability of your job because instead of judgment, you feel yourself to be surrounded by love.

WHEN YOU GIVE UP THE ILLUSION OF CONTROL, IT'S TRUE THAT YOU CAN'T ALWAYS STOP BAD THINGS FROM HAPPENING. BUT YOU CAN'T STOP GOOD THINGS FROM HAPPENING, EITHER.

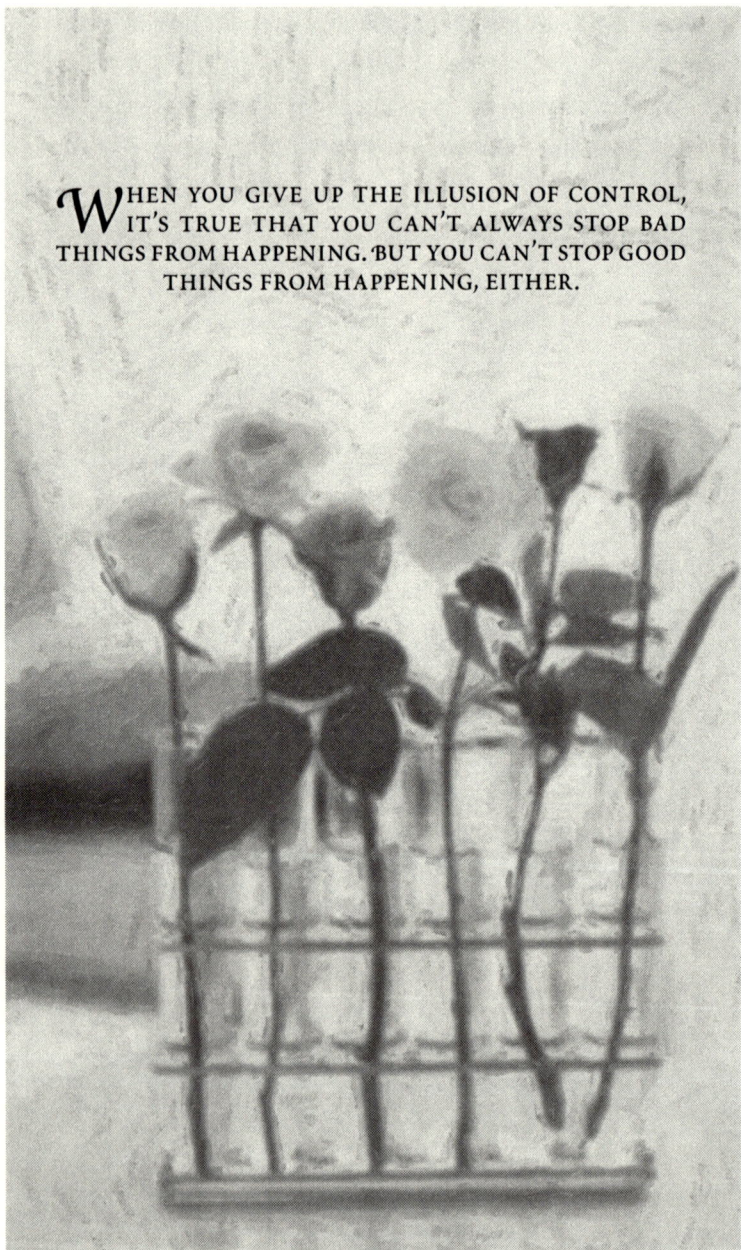

44

The only way I know how to get to this space is to live one's life day by day, come what may. I don't know how to make the good things happen, but I can keep putting one foot ahead of the other, trusting that good things will eventually start happening again. As much as I've been able to make out so far, that blessing comes as a by-product of one's audacious demand to live a life of meaning and the humility to know that controlling the outcome is not within your power, no matter how smart, hard-working, and deserving you are. I have found no easier way.

So: is it possible to keep one's spirit intact, even while losing your job, dealing with rejection and uncertainty, seeking a new way to make a living? The answer is yes. Do I wish I could have gotten to this place without enduring everything I had to endure? Yes again. Would I have preferred to have made this spiritual advancement by strolling along the seashore, hiking in the mountains and attuning myself to the whispers of conches? Yes, yes, and yes again.

And finally: given the good that came from all this, would I want to do it again? Not on your life.

So what about the year to come?

I don't have any guarantees, although I've struggled hard to get to a place where I can once again hope for the best. And what I really want hasn't changed since I began this year. I want to make a living and to be able to continue asking the big questions. But now I know that the answers can come both from the whisperings of conches and the buzz of fluorescent lights because all of life—even the disappointment and loss—takes place within God's loving embrace.

And so it is, a year after I set out to save my (downsized) soul that the memoir of this portion of my journey is nearly complete. In the end, I have to thank you—dear reader—for listening to my story. Whatever you are facing in your life, know that you are not alone and that the world needs you, too, now more than ever. But before we say goodbye for now, there is one more story.

Postscript

year after I set out to save my downsized soul, I decided to take Lucky for a drive. Lucky, you may recall, loves nothing better than to sit on my lap, her head poking out the open window.

We took the skyline route along Mulholland and turned a corner on the winding road, once again finding ourselves driving into a horizon ablaze in fire orange and red with streaks of ocean blue. I was again awestruck by the beauty of the blazing expanse—and something in my soul stirred to life.

This time, there was an overlook straight ahead. I pulled in and turned off the engine.

I knew this was a moment worth savoring.

And I did.

Ten Keys

1. ALL YOU CAN HOPE TO CONTROL, HOWEVER LONG YOU HAVE AND IN WHATEVER THE CIRCUMSTANCES, IS WHETHER YOU WILL BRING YOUR BEST OR WORST TO BEAR.

2. THERE ARE TIMES WHEN ALL YOU CAN DO IS REMEMBER TO BREATHE.

3. IT IS THE WILLINGNESS TO ENGAGE IN THE STRUGGLE FOR WHAT REALLY MATTERS THAT MERITS GOD'S INTERVENTION—NOT HOW DESERVING YOU THINK YOU ARE, NOR WHETHER YOU MANAGE TO EMERGE UNWOUNDED.

4. BECAUSE OUR FUTURES ARE OPEN AND FREE, MANY INFLUENCES CONTRIBUTE TO HOW OUR LIVES WILL UNFOLD OVER TIME. IRONICALLY, OUR ABILITY TO HOPE BECOMES ONE OF THOSE FACTORS, CARRYING JUST ENOUGH WEIGHT TO MAKE THE DIFFERENCE.

5. NOT EVERYTHING THAT HAPPENS IS A MESSAGE. SOMETIMES A RAT IS ONLY A RAT.

...to Saving Your (downsized) Soul

6. EMBRACE THE POSSIBILITY THAT MANY THINGS ARE BOUND TO GET IN YOUR WAY. SUCCESS COMES NOT IN SPITE OF THE THINGS THAT HAPPEN TO YOU BUT BECAUSE YOU HAVE GROWN LARGE ENOUGH TO EMBRACE IT ALL.

7. IT IS IN THE VOID THAT THE STATUS QUO HAS THE LIGHTEST HOLD ON US. RELEASED FROM THE CONSTRUCTS OF OUR EVERYDAY LIFE, WE HAVE THE LEAST TO LOSE. IN THE VOID, WE ARE FREEST TO MAKE CHANGES.

8. YOU DON'T NEED AN UPBEAT OR EVEN A BRAVE ATTITUDE TO MAKE PROGRESS. YOU JUST NEED DISCIPLINE, PUTTING RESUMES OUT, MAKING PHONE CALLS, FOLLOWING UP LEADS AND THE LIKE. THIS YOU CAN DO HAPPY OR SAD, ANXIOUS OR FULL OF FAITH.W

9. IT'S THE ECONOMY THAT'S BROKEN, NOT YOU.

10. WHEN YOU GIVE UP THE ILLUSION OF CONTROL, IT'S TRUE THAT YOU CAN'T ALWAYS STOP BAD THINGS FROM HAPPENING. BUT YOU CAN'T STOP GOOD THINGS FROM HAPPENING, EITHER.

Sources

As a key aspect of my search for soul, I set out to put my core spiritual theories to the test. I found that many of the inspirational teaching stories I'd gathered during the thirty-year span of my writing career had happily stood the test of time. Original and expanded versions, plus many more, can be found in the following.

The Art of Resilience: 100 Paths to Wisdom and Strength in an Uncertain World.
New York: Three Rivers Press/Random House, 1997.

Boom: Marketing to the Ultimate Power Consumer—the Baby Boomer Woman. With Mary Brown. New York: Amacom Publishing, 2006.

How Would Confucius Ask for a Raise? New York: William Morrow, 1993 and New York: Avon Books, 1994.

Inner Excellence: A Book About Meaning, Spirit and Success. New York: Amacom Publishing, 1999.

"Integrity in Business." In *The Soul of Business.* Ed. Charles Garfield. New York: Hay House, 1997.

Nothing Left Unsaid: Words to Help You and Your Loved Ones Through the Hardest Time.
Berkeley, California: Conari Press, 2001.

The Silver Pearl: Our Generation's Journey to Wisdom. With Dr. Jimmy Laura Smull. Chicago: Ampersand, Inc., 2005.

Solved by Sunset: The Self-Guided Intuitive Decision-Making Retreat. New York: Harmony, 1996 and New York: Crown, 1997.

Speak the Language of Healing (with Dr. Susan Kuner et al.) Berkeley, California: Conari Press, 1997.

Sources by others referenced in this memoir:

Man's Search for Meaning. Frankl, Viktor. Boston: Beacon Press, 1962.

The Holy Scriptures. Philadelphia: The Jewish Publication Society of America, 1917.

The I Ching. Wilhelm, Richard, and Baynes, Cary F. Foreword by Carl Jung. Princeton, New Jersey: Princeton University Press, 1950.

Journal of a Solitude. Sarton, May. New York: W.W. Norton, 1973.

A Passion for Truth. Heschel, Abraham Joshua. New York: Farrar, Straus and Giroux, 1973.

The Power of Myth. Campbell, Joseph and Moyers, Bill, Ed. Betty Sue Flowers. New York: Doubleday, 1988.

Scarred by Struggle, Transformed by Hope. Chittister, Joan. Grand Rapids, Michigan: William B. Eerdmans, 2003.

The Varieties of Religious Experience: A Study in Human Nature. James, William. Introduction by Reinhold Niebuhr. New York: Collier Books, 1961.

Work's a Bitch and Then You Make it Work. Kay, Andrea. New York: Harry N. Abrams, 2008.

Interview with the Author

Questions posed by Stephen Reily, Founder and CEO of VibrantNation.com

What moved you to write this memoir?

I began the year of saving my (downsized) soul thinking that I had recklessly broken my very core. My own salvation began the moment I took up my pen every night after my long days at work to record my experiences. I instinctively knew I needed to do something to make sense of what was happening to me. While I'd written 15 books over the past 25 years, many of them inspirational and advice books, this was not a work I intended for publication. I literally wrote this book to save my soul—and it wasn't until the year I set out to save my (downsized) soul was nearly over that I thought to share this with Patti Breitman, an old friend, and my former agent, wondering if there might be something in this for others. Outside of my own personal journals, I'd never written anything so exposed. Had I shown too much of myself? Her response excited and alarmed me. "This is a brave book" were her exact words.

In what ways is this book a departure from your previous books that were primarily centered in the self-help genre?

The main reason I ended up in corporate life, in the first place, was that I had put my writing career behind me and I needed to find a new way to make a living. It's not that I didn't love being an author—I always feel most passionate about life when immersed in the writing process. But I felt that a new time was dawning for authors and readers, alike. The era of authority telling us how we ought to live our lives is definitively over. What we crave, rather, is personal experience, to touch it and feel it—not principles shared from the top down, but the raw, gritty stuff of the fully-lived life.

How are things going for you with your career now?

The same ethos that propelled the writing of this memoir continues to make my role as Senior Strategist with VibrantNation.com such a great fit for me. For starters, I really enjoy my relationships with the team at Vibrant Nation. Each of us is mission-driven, bringing the best we have to work with us every day. In terms of the site itself, I love the easy and meaningful exchanges available to me when and where I most want to contribute to or access the communal wisdom of like-minded women. In addition, I believe that social networking is the embodiment of the anti-authoritarian spirit this memoir represents. Now that I've tasted sharing this level of personal experience, I view my participation in Vibrant Nation as the evolution of my own career, as well as an indication of the irrepressible trajectory of my generation of women.

Thanks for sharing about your book and career. Now I'd like to ask you four questions we like to pose to members on our site. The first is: How did you get to where you are now?

The easy answer is: one well-meaning decision at a time. Some were good, some not so good—but each one represented the best I could bring to the party at the moment. In other words, I have been working hard over the years to develop compassion for myself and others—a hard-won trait for a perfectionist who spent the first half of her life believing that if only I worked hard enough, tried hard enough, and lost those last ten pounds, I could master my destiny.

Of course, life had other plans for me. Career, family, parenting, health or relationships, I've been near the peak of the mountain and into the void numerous times. Somehow, I always bounce back—and usually a little higher than the last go-round, which does, in retrospect, represent some kind of progress. In fact, if there is any trait that has served me best to help me get to where I am now, it is my ability to learn from my mistakes. And another, closely related: my belief that this is a loving universe.

How do you see yourself differently now than you did 10 years ago?

Ten years ago, pursuing my Ph.D. in religious studies at Vanderbilt University, I was at the same time undergoing and recuperating from a life-threatening illness. While others stressed over their studies, exams, and dissertation, I was praying only to remember always what a gift life is. I recall taking long walks with friends, smelling flowers as if for the first time, radiating love to my kids, husband, professors, and even total strangers.

As it became increasingly apparent that I was going to live, fully recovered, I began losing some of the spiritual glow. Everyday life, with all the responsibilities, stresses, expectations, came trickling, tumbling, and then ultimately gushing back in. My prayer, to remember that life is a gift, has now become my mission: not so much a goal as it is the ground of being from which I operate. Having experienced so many extremes, I am full of paradoxes. I am stronger and more vulnerable, more compassionate and better able to set boundaries, full of faith and far more discriminating, living for the moment and more aware of mortality.

Where do you see yourself in 10 years?

On a good day: when projecting into the future, I remind myself that I will still be me. I love to read, write, think, teach, and mentor, and I expect to be doing so ten, twenty and maybe even forty years from now. For better (and sometimes for worse) I love giving advice, unsolicited or not. I'm sure I'll be "working," but already, the line between work and passion has become blurry indeed. I imagine that ten years from now, I'll be that much wiser, proficient and valuable, and that there will be an increased demand for what I have to offer.

My family and friends have only become increasingly important to me over time. By then, I will have grandchildren (my son and daughter-in-law are expecting now) and see myself surrounded by love and laughter.

Not that I won't, of course, be dealing with diminishments. But that's nothing new. I remember when I turned 35 and needed glasses for reading for the first time. I cried a bunch, realizing that once something like the ability to read without glasses is gone, it may not come back. Of course I adapted. Now I think of my glasses as a fashion statement.

I have an excellent model for all this, by the way. My sister-in-law, Sue Stein, is nearly ten years older than me and full of vitality and life. In fact, her greatest asset is her ability to laugh at herself. Ever since she came into the family, she has been a way-shower, always ten years ahead, and always lighting the way. I hope to do the same for the younger women in my life and in my world.

On a bad day:

Pry the 401k statement out of my fingers, pass the hanky, and uncork a nice bottle of wine.

Finally, if you could send a postcard to your younger self, what would you write?

Dear Younger Self,

Greetings from the new frontier, where I am journeying through previously unmapped territory, in both my heart and world.

You would love it here, although much of it is so unexpected. I do love an adventure, though, as long as I have the right supplies, and, of course, the faith that it will turn out all right in the end.

Thanks so much for the gift of the flashlight that functions in the darkest voids, and I still have the flag you gave me to plant the moment I finally reach the top of the mountain.

Thanks, too, for all the hard work you put into making this trip possible. And please don't worry about us so much. We're going to be fine.

Love,
Me Now

How would you answer these last four questions about yourself? We'd love to know!
Please visit www.VibrantNation.com

About the Author

Dr. Carol Orsborn is an author, marketing veteran and thought leader on issues related to Boomer women, adult development and quality of life. Carol serves as VibrantNation.com's senior strategist and blogs regularly for the peer-to-peer information-sharing website for women 50+. Carol has previously served as senior partner with a marketing-to-Boomer-woman firm affiliated with a top ten advertising agency, as senior vice president with a global public relations company and as co-founder of an international initiative dedicated to internal and external communications targeting the Boomer generation.

In the late 1980's, Carol founded the self-help organization *Superwomen's Anonymous*, a pioneer of the simplicity, life balance and business consciousness movements. Carol is the author of 15 books on generation-based issues in work and life, including *Boom: Marketing to the Ultimate Power Consumer—The Baby Boomer Woman* (Mary Brown/Carol Orsborn) and *The Art of Resilience* (Three Rivers Press).

Speaking to and for her generation, she has appeared on *Oprah* and *The Today Show*, and in the pages of *People Magazine* and *The New York Times*.

Carol received her Ph.D. from Vanderbilt University and has served on the faculties of Georgetown University, Vanderbilt University's Leadership Development Center of the Owen Graduate School of Management, and the Doctoral Program in Organizational Leadership at Pepperdine University's Graduate School of Education and Psychology. Carol, husband Dan, and dog Lucky live in Los Angeles, California. She is the proud mother of two adult children, enjoying her growing extended family.

An Invitation to Join VibrantNation.com

Carol Orsborn invites you to become a member of
VibrantNation.com, the first peer-to-peer information-
sharing website devoted exclusively to women 50+
who share the desire to make the most of life every day.
VibrantNation.com is our place online where we can
exchange information and join in smart conversation on
everything from the best beauty products for women 50+,
wellness and dating to reinvention, parenting adult children,
travel experiences and more. VibrantNation.com is also
where you can share your own stories about how you are
saving your own (downsized) soul and discuss this memoir
with others.

VibrantNation.com is the brainchild of founder/CEO
Stephen Reily, a marketer who shares the belief that
stereotypes have for many years kept the business and
societal mainstream from appreciating not just the size of
our pocketbooks but also the level of our connectedness.

For free membership, visit www.VibrantNation.com.

An Invitation to Contact Carol Orsborn

carol@vibrantnation.com
Follow Carol Orsborn on Twitter @CarolOrsborn
HTTP://Twitter.com/CarolOrsborn

Vn books

Breinigsville, PA USA
29 October 2009
226620BV00001B/5/P